Take-Home/ Keep-at-Home Books

VOLUME 2

TO ACCOMPANY

FULL SAILS
AND ALL SMILES

Harcourt Brace & Company
Orlando Atlanta Austin Boston San Francisco Chicago Dallas New York Toronto London

SIGNATURES

Printed in the United States of America

ISBN 0-15-307472-8

3 4 5 6 7 8 9 10 022 99 98 97

C O N T E N T S

Grade 1/Volume 2

Harcourt Brace School Publishers

TAKE-HOME/KEEP-AT-HOME BOOK

Full Sails

Use with "The Little Red Hen."

HARCOURT BRACE & COMPANY

Cap Gets a Garden

by Beverley Dietz

Now Cap and I have a garden of our own.
"Do you like this garden?" I asked Cap. I think he does!

One day my dog Cap and I went for a walk.
We walked up and down the block.
What do you think we found?

We found a plant!

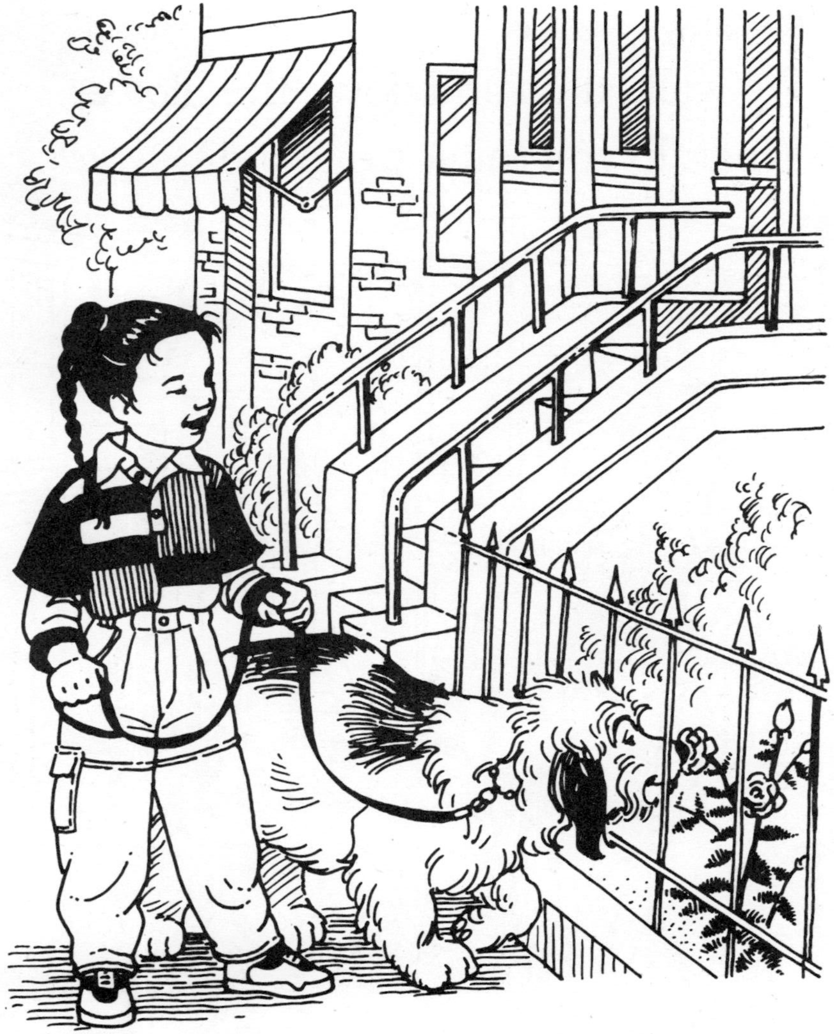

The next day, what do you think we did?

Harcourt Brace School Publishers

Dad and I went out. Cap came too.
"We could plant a garden here," I said.
"Cap can help."
Dad just looked at me. Then Cap
began to dig.

"Now I see!" said Dad. "Cap *does* want
a garden!" Then Dad and I began to
help Cap dig.

Then we saw some little gardens.
"Look at these plants," I said.
"Do you like this garden?" I asked.
I think he did.

Harcourt Brace School Publishers

We saw some gardens up high.
"Look at these plants," I said.
"This is a window garden." Cap looked.
"Do you like this garden?" I asked.
I think he did.

"Cap likes gardens?" asked Dad. "Cap is a dog. What makes you think Cap wants a garden?"
"Let's go out," I said. "You will see. Cap likes gardens." Cap looked happy.

"How can I help?" I asked Dad.
"Just mix this flour for me," he said.
I began to mix the flour.
Cap watched me.

"Cap and I went for a walk," I said.
"Oh?" Dad said.
"We saw some gardens," I went on.
"I think Cap likes gardens. Do you think we could have our own garden?"

We saw some big gardens.
"Look at these plants," I said.
"These plants are for eating."
Cap looked at the plants.
"Do you like this garden?" I asked.
I know Cap did! He wanted to go into the garden.
"Come on, Cap," I said. "These plants are not for you to eat!"

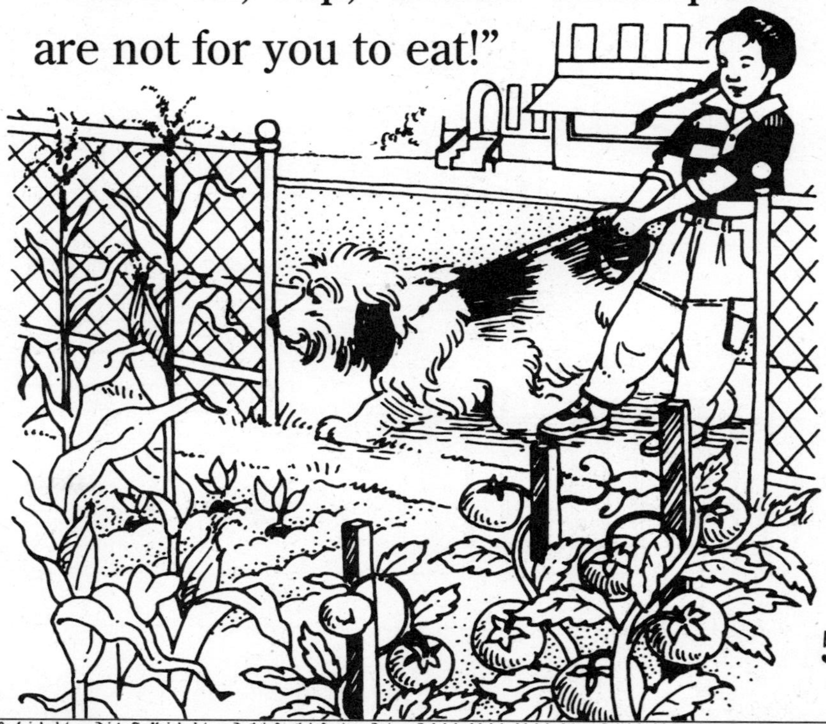

Cap and I walked back to our house.
What do you think we didn't see?
We didn't see a garden!
We didn't have one.

Dad came out to look for me.
He found me sitting with Cap. We did not look happy.
"Who can help me?" asked Dad.
"I can," I said.
I went into the house. Cap came with me. He likes to help, too.

Harcourt Brace School Publishers

TAKE-HOME/KEEP-AT-HOME BOOK

Full Sails

Use with "Henny Penny."

HARCOURT BRACE & COMPANY

by Annette King

Harcourt Brace School Publishers

"I know this, too," said the cow.
"When you are out walking and you find a sack, don't look into it!"
And they were both happy from then on.

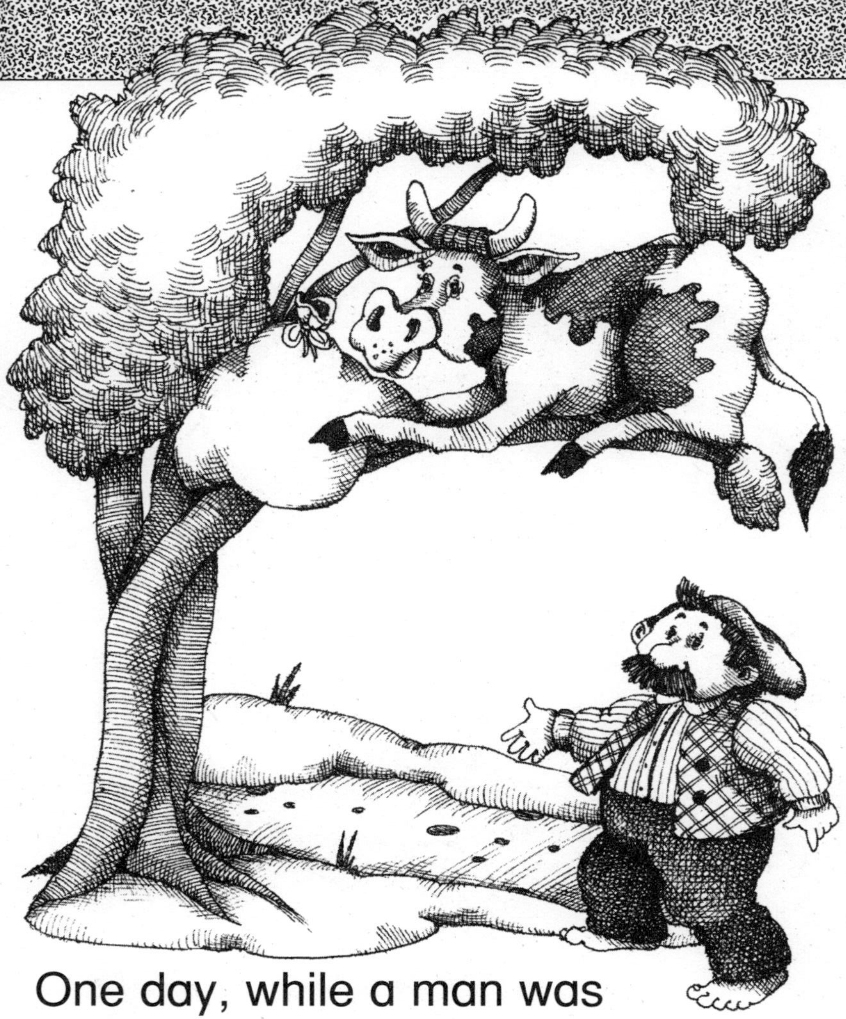

One day, while a man was out walking, he found a cow sitting on the branch of a big, old oak.
"What is this!" said the man.
"How could a cow get up in this oak?"

Harcourt Brace School Publishers

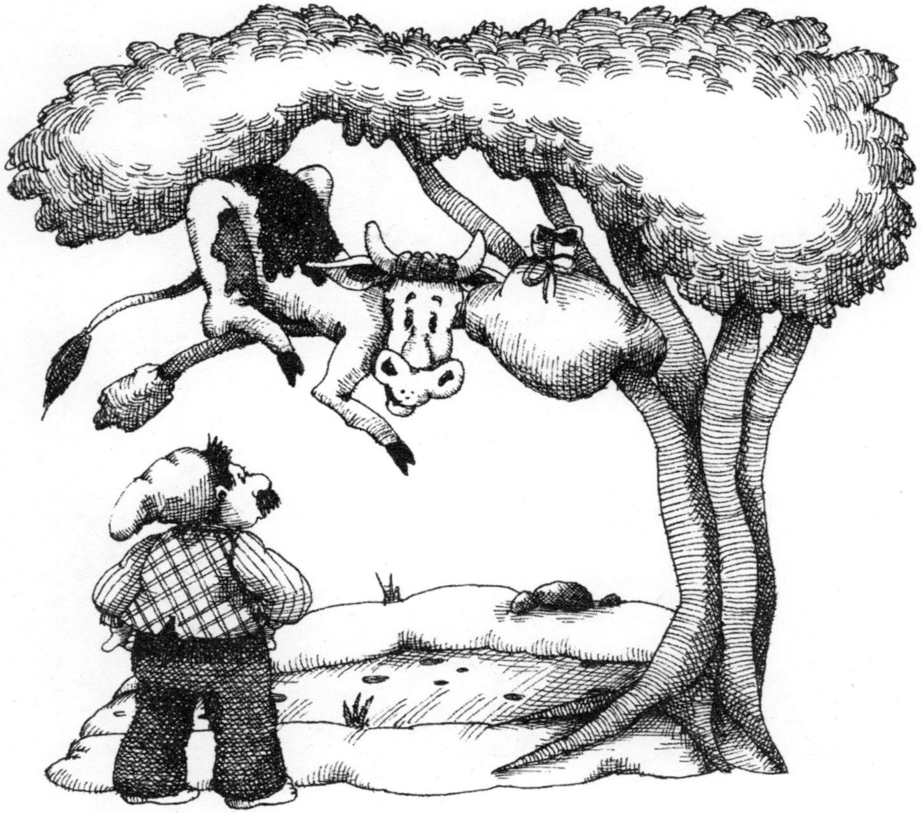

"It is not a happy story," said the cow.
"I found this sack, and I looked into it.
Then, surprise!
I was in the top of this oak!"

The man helped the cow climb down.
"Look, Cow!" he said. "My house is back, and no garden is on my head!"
"I know," said the cow. "You have found that troubles go away when you help a friend."

Harcourt Brace School Publishers

Then he said, "I will help you, Cow. But when you come down, you must help me. You and your sack must go away so my troubles will stop."

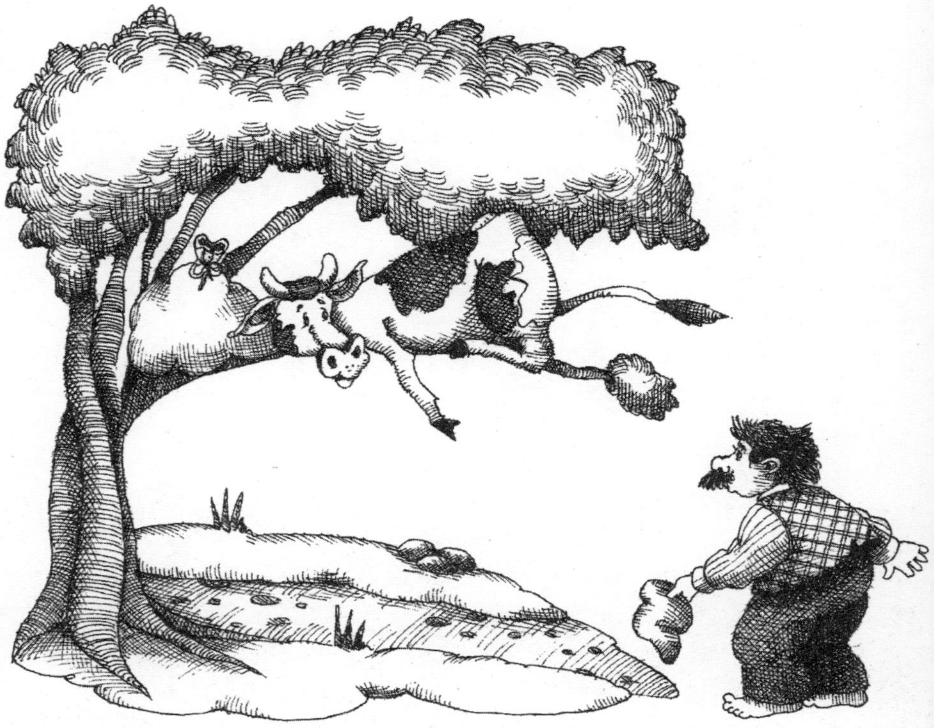

"This sack is a sack of trouble," the cow went on.

"Will you help me get down?"

"Oh, no," said the man.

"I can't help you."

"Why not?" asked the cow.

Harcourt Brace School Publishers

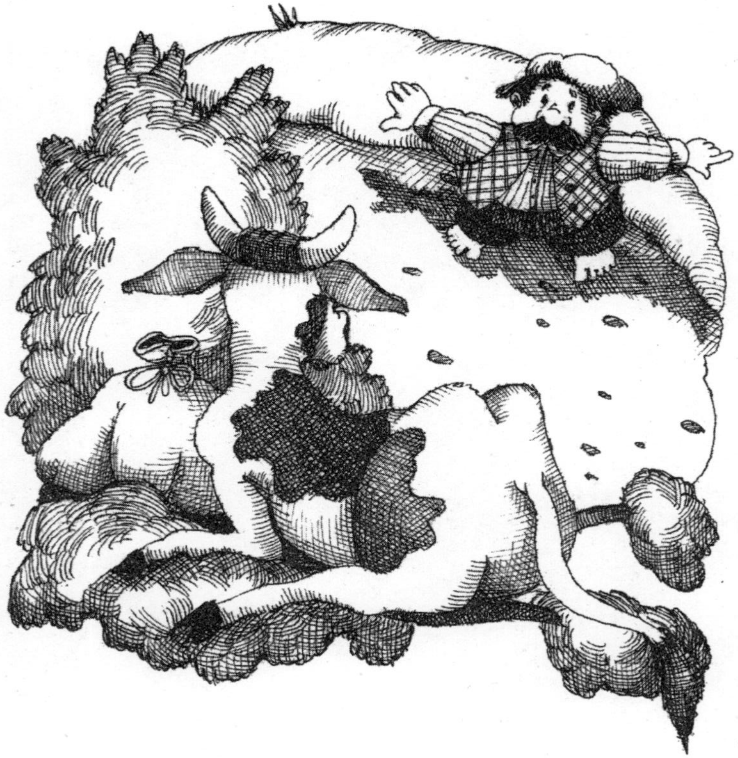

"You say the sack is a sack of trouble," said the man.
"The trouble in the sack could get out. It could get me! I don't want any trouble."
The man walked on.

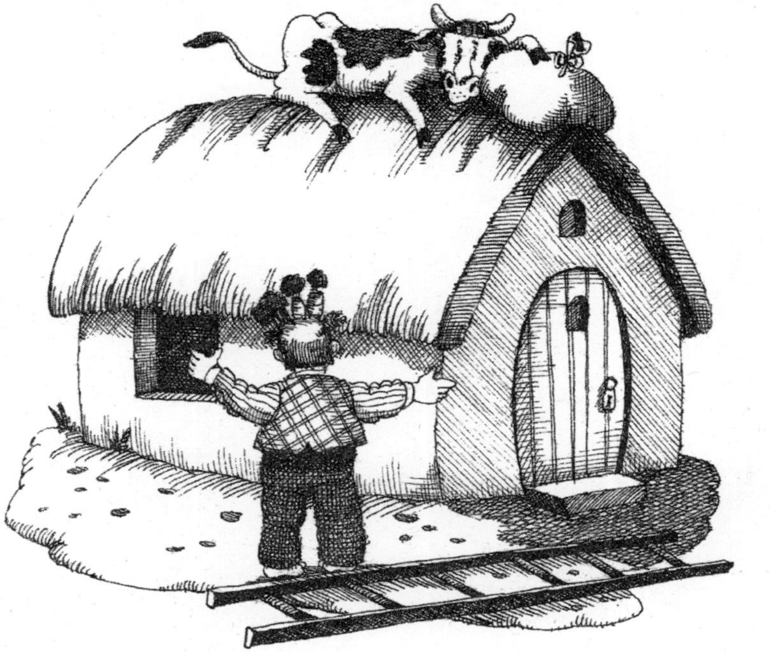

At last, the man found the cow.
She was sitting on top of his house—with the sack of troubles.
"Cow!" said the man. "What is my house doing here? And look at my head. A garden is growing on it! You must go away where the trouble in the sack can't find me."

The next day when the man got up, he looked up at the sky and said, "Where is my house?"

"This is the doing of the cow and the sack," said the man.

"I must look for the cow to get my house back and to get this garden off my head, too!"

The next day when the man woke up, he found a surprise. On his head was a garden!

"Oh, no!" he said. "The cow with the sack did this to me. I must find the cow to stop this trouble!"

Harcourt Brace School Publishers

When the man found the cow, she was sitting on top of a horse—with her sack of trouble.
"Cow!" said the man. "Look at my head! You must go away where the trouble in your sack can't find me."

"How can I go away?" asked the cow. "I'm on top of this horse! Will you help me get down?"
"No! No!" said the man. "I can't help you. I don't want any more trouble!"

TAKE-HOME/KEEP-AT-HOME BOOK

Full Sails

Use with "Little Lumpty."

HARCOURT BRACE & COMPANY

Rella Rabbit's Troubles

by Susannah Brin

Now every rabbit in Rabbit Town is happy. Now everybody is playing and dancing together outside in the King's garden.

But once in a while, Rella Rabbit still looks up at the top of the hill. What do you think she is thinking?

Rabbit Town was a happy place.

The little town was in the King's big garden. Everybody played and danced all day long.

Almost every rabbit was very happy.

Only one rabbit was not.

Harcourt Brace School Publishers

Rella Rabbit was not happy. She did not go outside. She did not play. All she did was look out the window in her room.

"What will make you happy?" asked Mother Rabbit.

"I want to see what is over the hill," said Rella.

Rella climbed back up the hill. She could see the King's garden and her little town.

"I'm almost home!" she said. And then down the hill she went. She did not stop. She just wanted to get home.

Out came Rella, out of the house.
Off went the dog, and the duck, and the bee.
Together, they all went after Rella.

"Oh, dear," said Mother. "You will only find trouble over the hill. You can't go until you grow up. You are too little."
Rella Rabbit did not think she was too little. She still wanted to go.

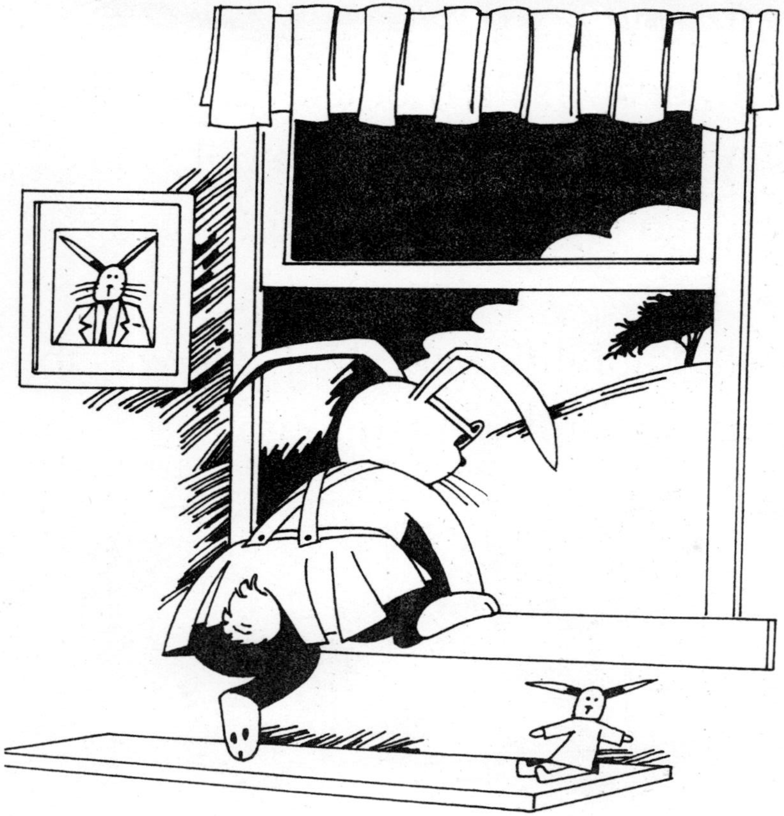

The next day, before the sun was up, Rella climbed out the window. "This is the best time to go. No one will see me," said Rella. And off she went.

Rella found a house, and in she went. "They can't catch me now," said Rella. Just then, a big dog said, "Get out of my home!"

"Oh, oh!" said Rella. "More trouble!"

Up jumped Rella, out of the lake.
Off went the duck, and off went the bee.
Together, they both went after Rella.

Rella climbed up to the top of the hill and looked down. She could see the King's garden and her town.
"I'm here," said Rella, "and I did not find any trouble! I just found a big, old oak."
Just then a big bee came flying out of the oak.

Harcourt Brace School Publishers

"Get away from my home!" said
the bee.
"Oh, oh!" said Rella. "I think this
is trouble!"
Off went Rella, away from the oak.
Off went the bee, after Rella.

Rella did not see the lake in time.
"Oh, no! I'm going to fall!" said Rella.
And she did.
"Quack!" said a duck. "Get out of
my home."
"Oh, oh!" said Rella. "More trouble!"

Harcourt Brace School Publishers

TAKE-HOME/KEEP-AT-HOME BOOK

Full Sails

Use with "The Wild Woods."

HARCOURT BRACE & COMPANY

Wild Animals

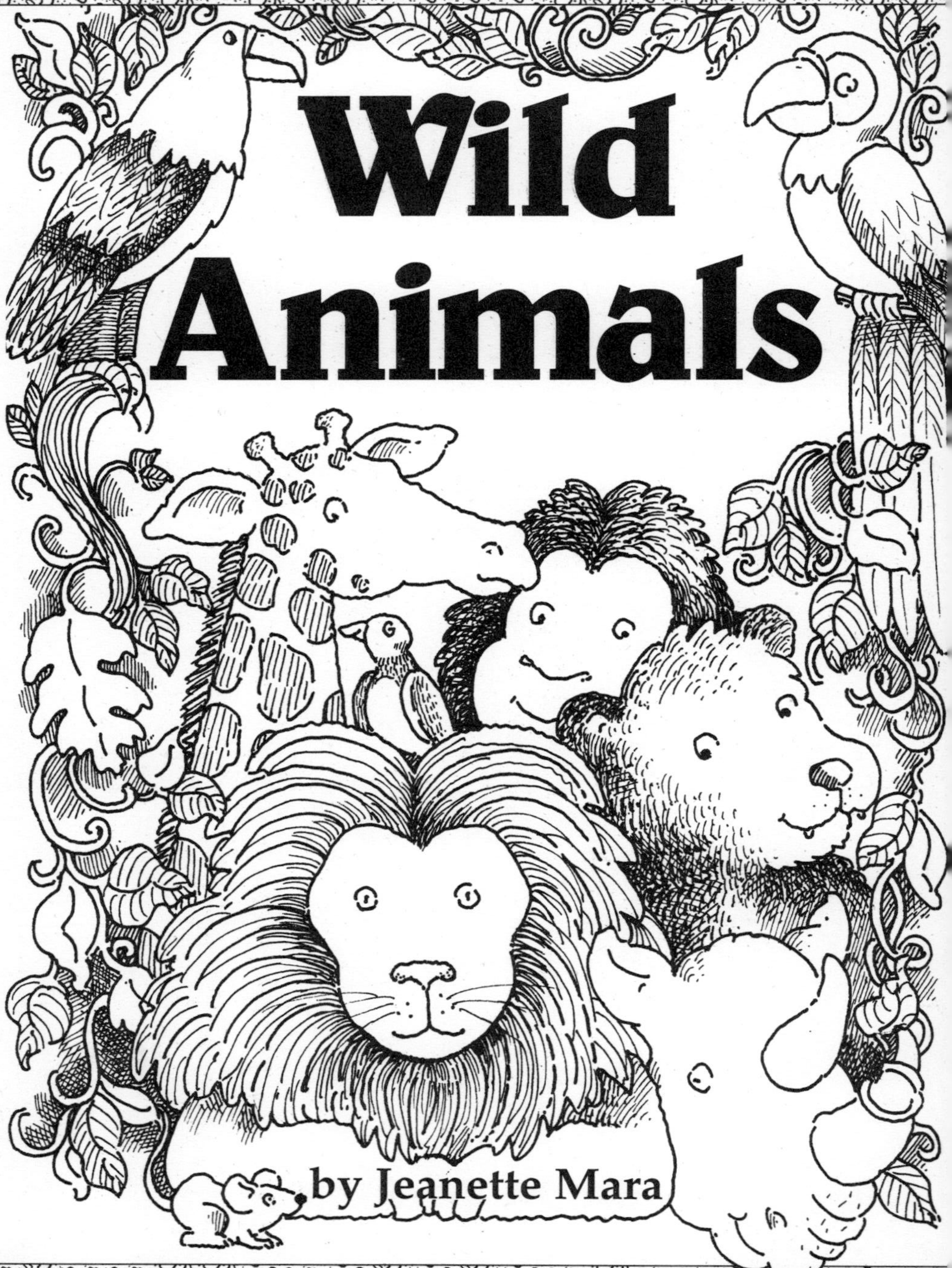

by Jeanette Mara

Look! You might see them, too!

My friend Ben likes animals. He likes little animals. He likes big animals. He likes house pets. But best of all, Ben likes wild animals.

Harcourt Brace School Publishers

One day I was outside playing with my dog. I looked up and saw Ben. "Do you want to help me make some wild animals?" he whispered. "What did you say?" I asked. "Do you want to help me make some wild animals?" This time he shouted.

We all went to the lake. "Surprise!" said Ben. "Here are some wild animals we can eat while we look for more wild animals!"

Ben called our friends.
"We have a surprise for you,"
he said. "Come to the lake, but
watch out for the wild animals."

"Wild animals?" I said. "You can't
make wild animals!"
"Oh, yes, I can," said Ben. "Come
with me. We will make sandwiches."
"Sandwiches?" I asked. "What do
sandwiches have to do with wild
animals?" I went with Ben because
I wanted to find out.

Harcourt Brace School Publishers

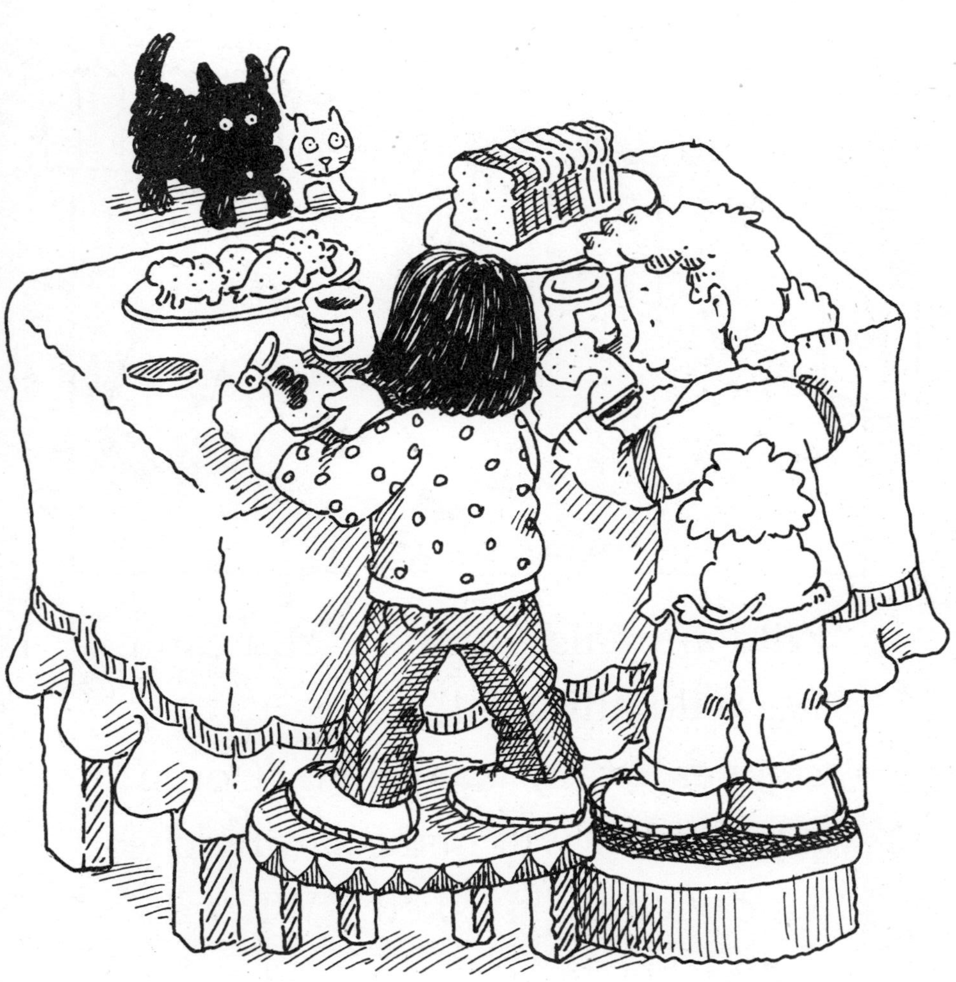

I helped Ben make the sandwiches.

Ben and I looked at all
our wild animal sandwiches.
"What will we do with all
of these?" I asked. "We can't
eat them all, and we can't
keep them all!"

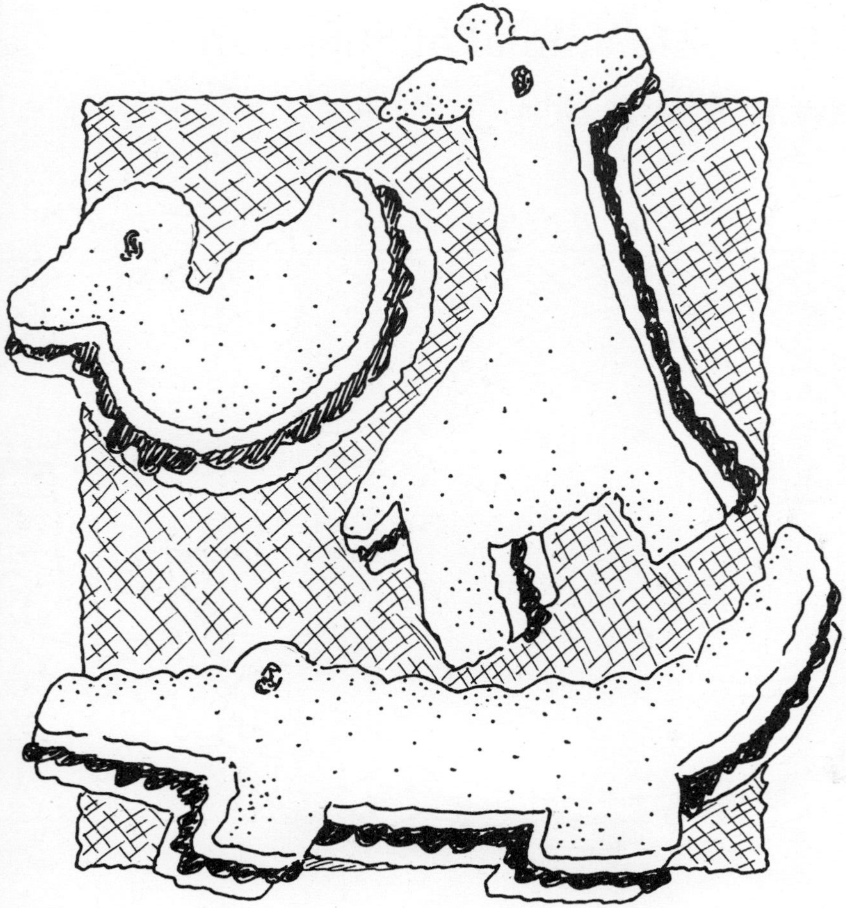

"Let's keep going!" said Ben.
"Let's make some more!"

"Now what?" I asked.
This is what Ben did.

"This is the wild animal
I like best," said Ben. "I like
it because it's a big cat!"

"What will you make?" Ben asked.
This is what I did.

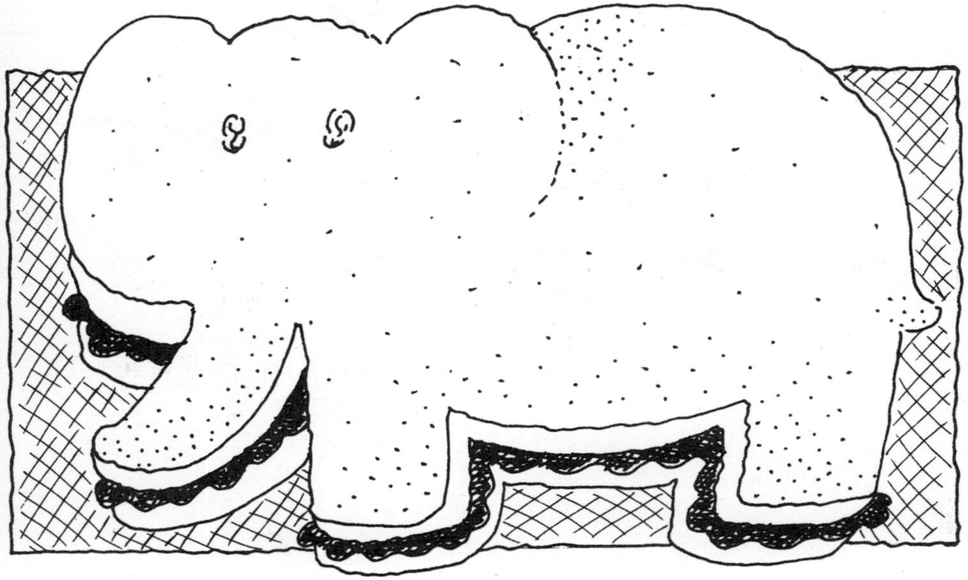

"Good!" shouted Ben. "I like the big trunk!"
"Let's make some more," I said.
"This is fun!"

"This wild animal might swim away," said Ben.

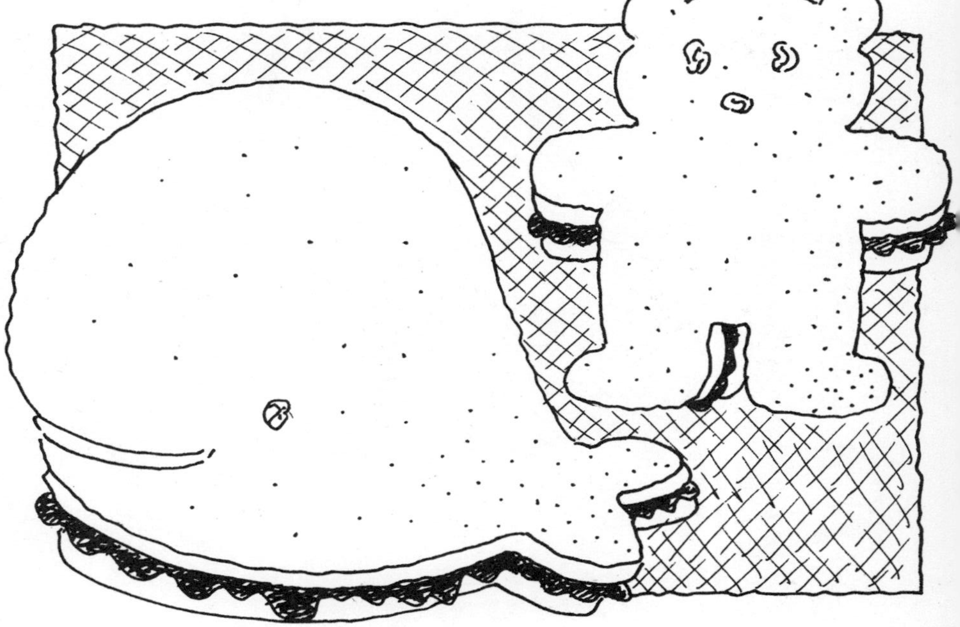

"My wild animal can swim, too," I said. "It can't climb up high, but I don't care. I like it!"

Harcourt Brace School Publishers

TAKE-HOME/KEEP-AT-HOME BOOK

Full Sails

Use with "Wonderful Worms."

HARCOURT BRACE & COMPANY

Jenny and the Flying Time

by Susannah Brin

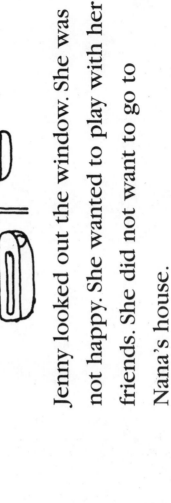

Then one day, when Jenny woke up, she found her mother and father outside. She was glad to see them. She was surprised, too.

"Why are you here?" she asked.

"Time to go home," said her mother.

"Home?" said Jenny. "But I just got here!"

"See," said everybody. "The time did fly!"

Jenny looked out the window. She was not happy. She wanted to play with her friends. She did not want to go to Nana's house.

"I know how you feel," said Jenny's mother, "but you will have so much fun, the time will fly."

Jenny didn't think so.

"You are going away for a very short time," said Jenny's mother.

"Only five days."

"Five days is a long time!" said Jenny.

"No, it's not. You will see. The time will fly," said her father.

Jenny didn't think so.

One day Jenny and Nana went for a boat ride. Jenny put her hand in the water.

"The water feels good," she said.

Harcourt Brace School Publishers

One day Jenny and her Nana walked over the hill to see Nana's friend. She had a pony. Jenny went for a ride on the pony while Nana and her friend watched.

Jenny was happy. She wasn't thinking about her friends back in town. It was fun at Nana's. And the time was flying.

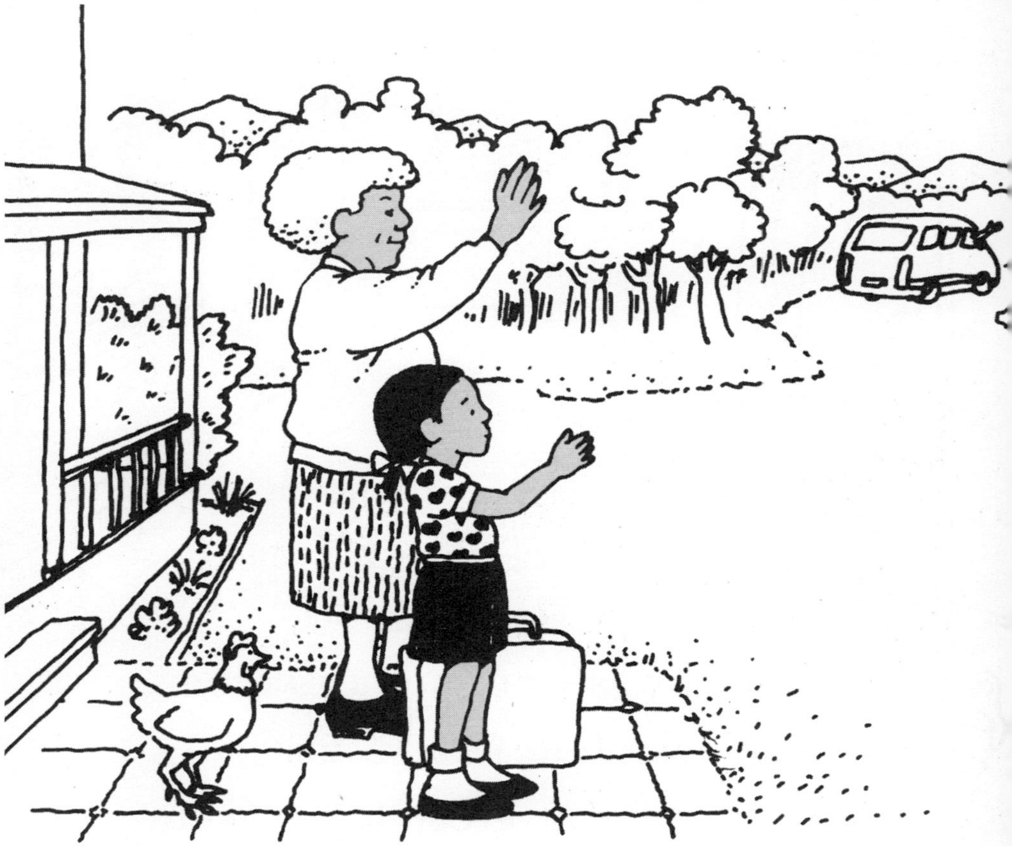

"I know how you feel," said Nana, "but we will have fun, and the time will fly."

Jenny still didn't think so.

Then she went into the house with Nana.

"This room was your mother's room when she was little," said Nana.
Big trees with soft, green leaves were growing next to the window.
"Your mother liked to watch the animals who live in these trees," said Nana.
"I like watching animals, too," said Jenny.

The next day, when Jenny got up, she found Nana in the garden. She was planting little green plants.
"Can I help?" asked Jenny.
"Yes, you can. Turn on the water," said Nana.
Jenny watered the little plants.

After watching the ducks, Jenny and
Nana went back to the house.
Sitting outside, they watched the sun
turn red.
"Why don't you live in town?"
asked Jenny.
"I like the way it is here," said Nana.
"I can see the sky and the hills."
"Yes," said Jenny. "This is a good place."

"Will the bird come soon?" asked Jenny.
"Oh, I think she will," said Nana.
Nana and Jenny watched the nest on
the big branch of the tree.

Nana and Jenny watched for the bird.
Soon, along came a big, red bird.
The bird had a worm.
"Here is the mother bird, and now I see three baby birds, too!" Jenny shouted.
"This is fun."
"Do you want to see more birds?" asked Nana.
"Oh, yes," said Jenny. "This is fun!"

They walked to the lake. Three ducks were in the water.
One duck was finding plants to eat.
Nana and Jenny watched the way ducks eat.
"This is fun!" said Jenny.

Harcourt Brace School Publishers

TAKE-HOME/KEEP-AT-HOME BOOK

Full Sails

Use with "Frog and Toad Together."

HARCOURT BRACE & COMPANY

Fly, Dilly! Fly!

by Erica Stanton

From then on, Dilly could fly.
And, the little duck is now a big duck like Dilly.
Now, when it is almost night, you can see them both flying all over the world.

Dilly was a duck.
He could do what most ducks do.
He could walk like a duck. He could swim like a duck. He could quack like a duck.
But Dilly couldn't fly like a duck.
He was afraid to fly.

Dilly Duck liked to swim.
Every day, Dilly played in the water with his friends.
But when it was almost night, Dilly's friends could fly up in the sky. Dilly could watch them fly, but Dilly could not fly with them.
Dilly felt too afraid to fly.

Up jumped the little duck on Dilly's back! Up jumped Dilly. Up into the sky went Dilly with the little duck.
"You can fly!" shouted the little duck.
"Look!" shouted Dilly. "I can fly!"

Dilly walked over the hill.
The little duck walked close to Dilly.
Then the little duck looked back.
"Look out! It's the fox!" shouted the little duck.

"I wish I could fly high up in the sky," Dilly said. "I can walk. I can swim. I can quack. But, oh, how I wish I could fly!"

"You can do it," said Dilly's mother. "Just do this." She jumped off the ground and went up, high into the sky. "You can do it," shouted Dilly's father, as he went over the trees.

"I will help you find your home. Walk close to me so the fox can't get you," said Dilly.

"I'm afraid of the red fox," said the little duck. "The red fox chased me all the way from my house. It was a long run for a little duck. Can you help me?"

Dilly jumped off the ground.

But he didn't go up into the sky. He didn't go over the trees.

Again, and again, he jumped off the ground. Again and again, he just came back down.

"All this work, and I still can't fly," he said.

Harcourt Brace School Publishers

One day, everybody but Dilly went up to fly in the sky. Dilly saw the bushes move. Looking into the bushes, Dilly saw a little duck.

"What are you doing here?" Dilly asked the little duck.

"I have to run away," said the little duck. "Can you help me?"

"Why?" asked Dilly. "Are you afraid?"

"Yes," said the little duck.

"I'm afraid, too," said Dilly. "I'm afraid to fly."

Harcourt Brace School Publishers

TAKE-HOME/KEEP-AT-HOME BOOK

Full Sails

Use with "Lionel in the Winter."

HARCOURT BRACE & COMPANY

My Two Friends

by Kelsey Brown

My mother and father said I could keep the cat. I called my cat Snowball. From then on, Red, Snowball, and I were always together.

When I was small, all my friends lived in town. So most of the time, I didn't have any friends to play with. One day, my father came home with a surprise. "I have a friend for you," he said. "This is Red."

Harcourt Brace School Publishers

I liked Red. I gave him a big hug.
"I wanted a friend," I said to Red.
"I'm glad you're going to live here.
Here is a scarf for you."

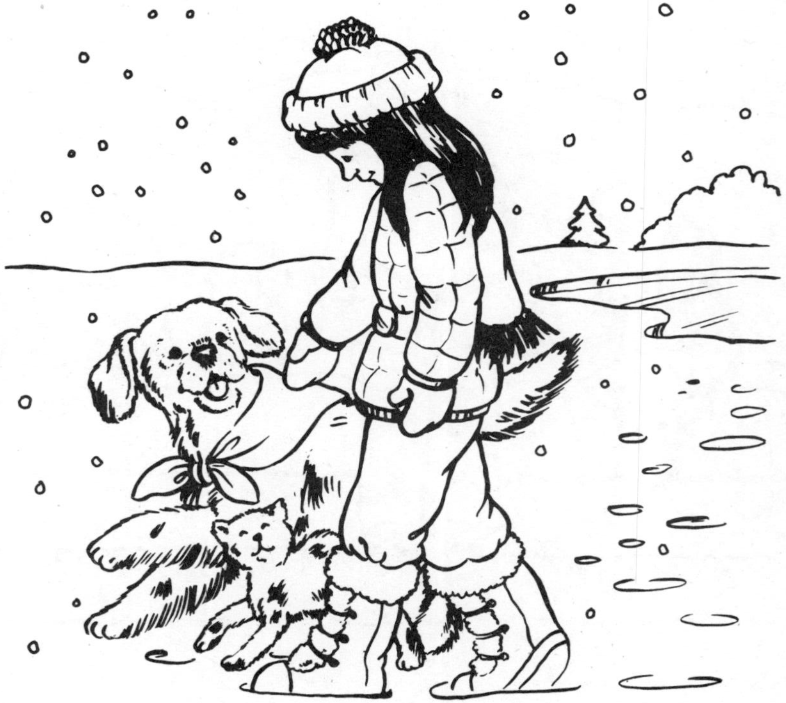

"I found you, Red!" I said.
"And you found the cat. You're a good dog, Red." Then the cat, Red, and I walked home.

I went to the lake.
Close to the lake, I saw our small boat.
I lifted up the boat. What do you think
I saw?
I saw my dog, Red.
Next to Red was the cat.

Soon Red and I were best friends. We went for long walks and climbed the hills together. We went to the lake. Red liked to play catch.

Harcourt Brace School Publishers

One day, while we were at the lake, we saw a small cat. Red chased after the cat. The cat looked at Red. Red was facing the cat. He jumped. The cat jumped, too, and went off up a tree.

I climbed the big hill. From the top
I could see my house.
Again, I shouted, "Red! Red!
Come here, Red!"

Harcourt Brace School Publishers

I shouted, "Red! Red!
Where are you? Come
here, Red!"
Red didn't come. Where
was Red?

We walked home as it began to snow.
I was thinking about the small cat.
It didn't have a good home like Red
and I have.
"It wasn't right to jump at the cat,"
I said.
Red looked at the ground.

Harcourt Brace School Publishers

Later Red and I sat on the end of my bed. We were facing the window and watching the snow fall.
I was still thinking about the cat.
When my father got home from work, Red went outside. He didn't come back.
After a while, I went to bed.

When I woke up,
I asked my mother, "Where is Red?"
"Red didn't come home last night," she said.
"Oh, no! Do you think he's in trouble?" I asked.
I went right out to look for him.

Harcourt Brace School Publishers

TAKE-HOME/KEEP-AT-HOME BOOK
Full Sails
Use with "Jenny's Journey."

HARCOURT BRACE & COMPANY

Dear Anna

by Ben Farrell

Harcourt Brace School Publishers

Dear Anna,
I'm home!
Let's play!
Your friend,
Pedro

Dear Anna,

I'm flying! And I like it! You were right. This is fun. I'm not afraid now. I like looking out the window. The sky is so blue. I can see a town on the ground. It looks so little from up here.

Your friend,

Pedro

Dear Anna,

It is morning now. We are still up in the sky. Soon our long ride will end. We will come back down to the ground.

I miss you.

Your friend,

Pedro

Dear Anna,

I'm going back up in the sky. We are off the ground and headed up. It will be a long ride. Now I know what I want to do when I grow up. Someday I want to fly a plane! I will see you soon.

Your friend,

Pedro

Dear Anna,

It is almost time to come home. I have only two more days. When I get home, we can play all day.

Your friend,

Pedro

Dear Anna,

This morning I went for a ride on a horse. I went to a small lake. I liked my ride. It was so much fun. I wanted to go on another ride. Someday I will.

Your friend,

Pedro

Dear Anna,

I wrote a story. It is about a dancing horse. The horse danced past a dancing cow. The horse did not like dancing all alone. Now the horse is happy. It is dancing with the cow.

Your friend,

Pedro

Dear Anna,

This morning I climbed, and I climbed, and I climbed. I can see all over from up here. I wish you were here, too. I'm having a good time.

Your friend,

Pedro

Dear Anna,

I'm glad you wrote to me. Did you have a happy birthday? How did you like your birthday cake? I miss you. I wish you were here.

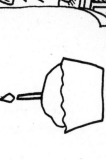

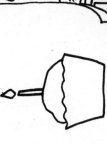

Your friend,

Pedro

Dear Anna,

I went to see the animals this morning. I saw the sheep, ducks, cows, and a horse. I liked the sheep the best. One of the sheep was a baby. It looked like this.

Your friend,

Pedro

Dear Anna,

Do you like boats? I went for a ride on a boat. The boat moved out into the open water. I saw a lot of fish.

Your friend,

Pedro

Dear Anna,

Look! I'm flying again! This is a wild way to fly. And it is so much fun. I don't want to come down to the ground. I just want to keep flying up here!

Your friend,

Pedro

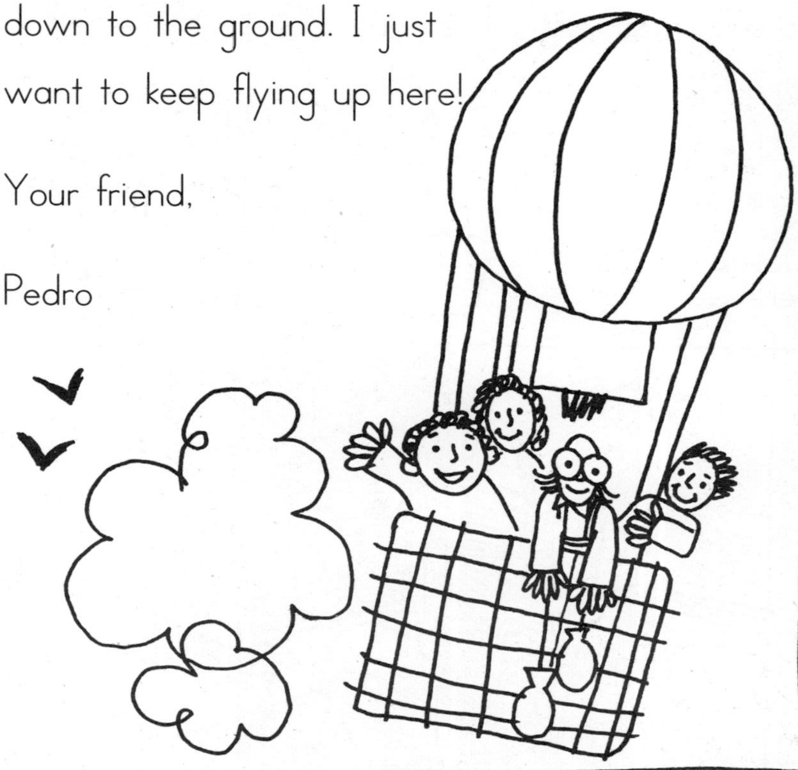

TAKE-HOME/KEEP-AT-HOME BOOK

All Smiles

Use with "Dreams."

HARCOURT BRACE & COMPANY

Shadows

by Beverley Dietz

Here is some more shadow fun.
What shadows will you make?

Someone is walking
down the street.
Do you see the shadow?
How big it is! Who could
have this big shadow?

It's me! I'm not big, but right now my shadow is. Later today, my shadow will get small—very small. Do you know why?

Look at this shadow. It looks like a bird trapped in someone's hand. But it's a shadow made with three hands.

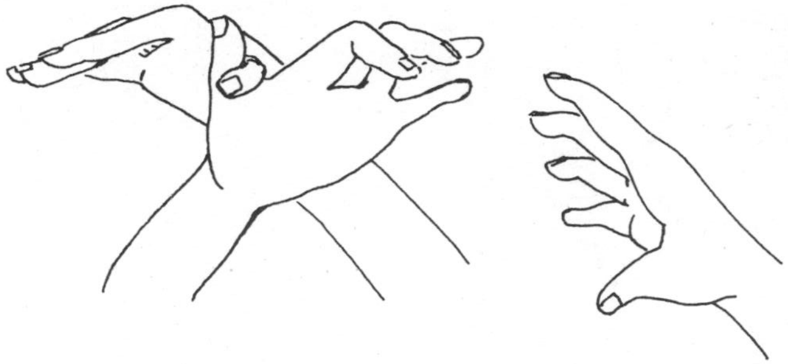

Do you know what animal this is?
How about this one?

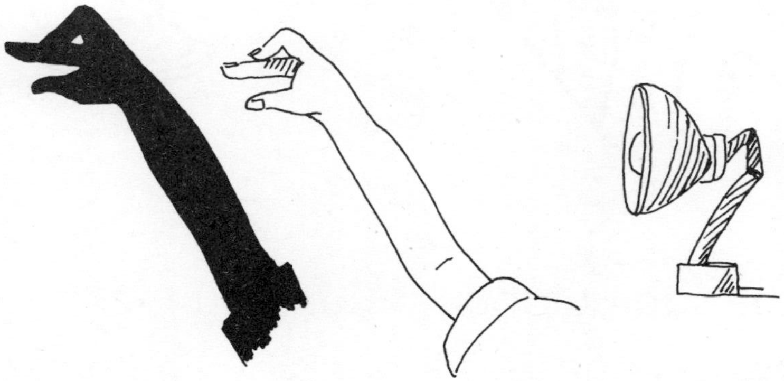

You can make these shadows, too!

Look in the sky. Where is the sun?
How do our shadows look?
Let's wait awhile and then look at our shadows again.

Where is the sun now? It's high in the sky, right over our heads. Look at our shadows now!

Look now! Our shadows grew big again.
Where is the sun now?

Is the sun out today? Can you make shadows outside? If not, you can make shadows in your school room.

A house made
this shadow.

A horse made
this shadow.

This is a shadow
of a window.

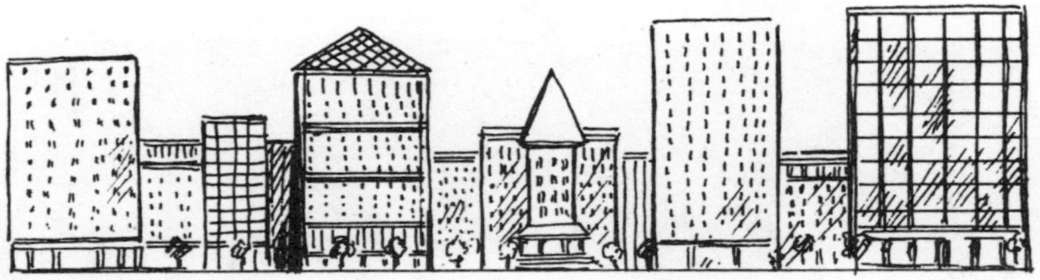

And this is a shadow of a city!

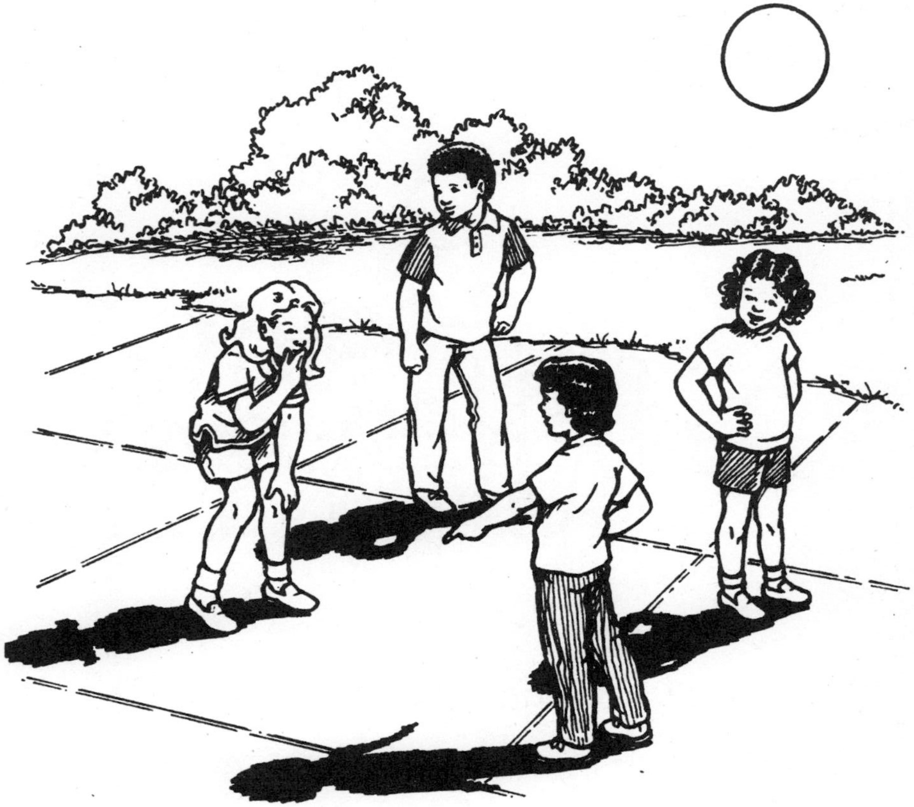

You make shadows, too.
When the sun is out, you make a shadow on the ground.
In the morning, your shadow is very big because of where the sun is.

Later in the day, your shadow is very small.

Later on, your shadow gets big again. Why? Because of the sun!

Let's have some fun. Look at these shadows. What do you think made them?

Harcourt Brace School Publishers

TAKE-HOME/KEEP-AT-HOME BOOK

All Smiles

Use with "Henry and Mudge in the Green Time."

HARCOURT BRACE & COMPANY

The King's Cape

by Jean Groce

So once more the sun came up every day. Everybody was glad.

The King put the shining cape back into the trunk. "I'll never put it on again," he said.

And he didn't.

One day three men were working in the King's garden. They found an old trunk and lifted it out of the ground. Then the men scrubbed the old trunk, and when they were done, one of them said, "Let's take it to the King!" This is just what they did.

When the King opened the trunk, he was very surprised. "Look at this," he shouted. "What a cape! It shines just like the sun. I almost have to close my eyes!"

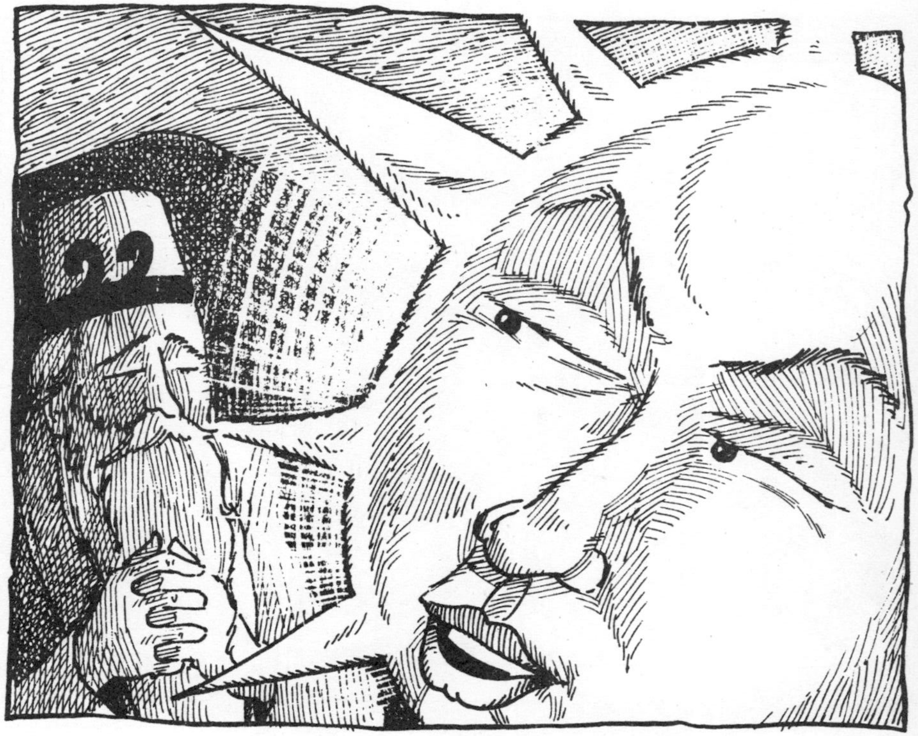

"No," said the King, shaking his head. "My cape shines only when you shine. Only you are the sun. I'll never again say you are not wanted."

The sun was happy now. It started to shine.

"Sun!" said the King. "At last I've found you. Could you shine for us once again?"

"Why?" asked the sun. "You said you didn't want me. You think you shine like I do. You make day come."

The King put on the cape. Then he walked all over town saying, "Look at me! I shine like the sun! Who could want the sun when I shine like this?"

Everybody looked at the King. "We do not want the sun," they said. "The sun never shined like our King!"

Up in the sky, the sun saw this and was not happy. "They think they do not want me, so I'll go away!" This is just what the sun did.

So the King went off to see the sun. He walked for days. He climbed up hill after hill. He climbed up as high as he could go.

At last the King came to some steps. When he climbed them, the King was at the top of the world! Here the King found the sun.

At last they went to see the King.

"Our eyes can't see in the night. We can't do our work. What will we do?"

"I don't shine like the sun after all," the King said. "I now know we have to have the sun. I will go and ask the sun to shine again."

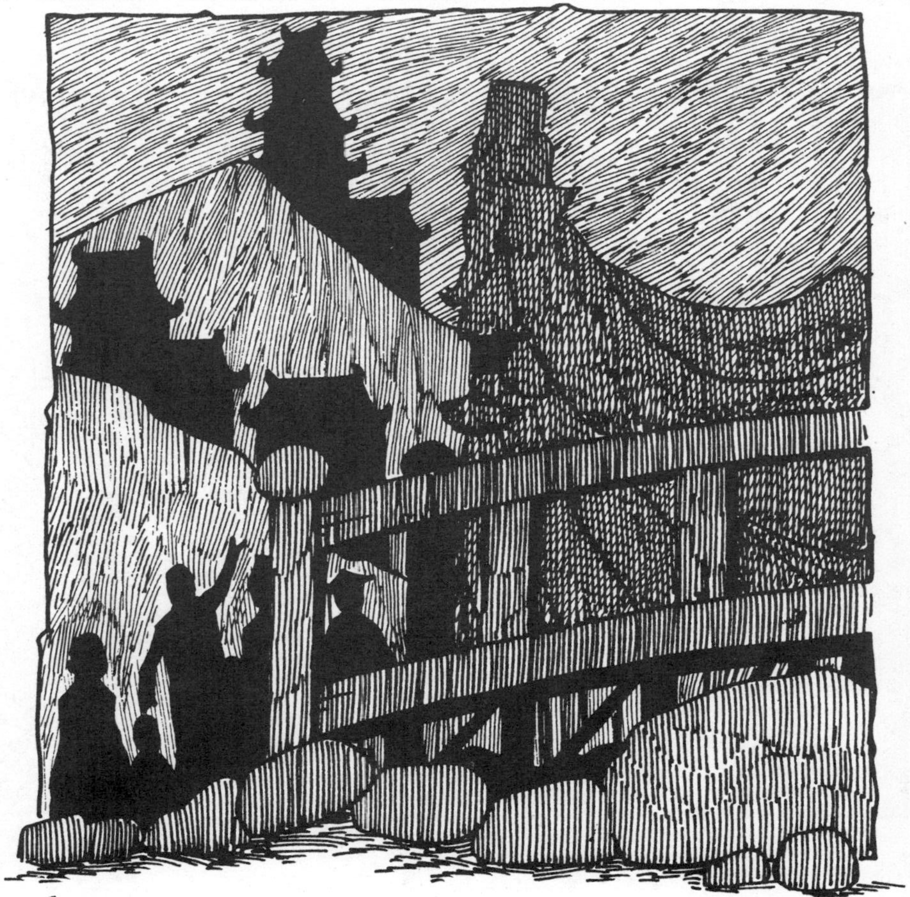

The next morning, the sun did not come up. It was night all day long. The King put on his cape, but it did not shine in the night.

"Look!" everybody said. "It is night all day! What fun! We will not have to get up in the morning. And here is the best part. We will not have to work! We can just play and play all day!"

It was always night. Soon, having night all day was not fun. No one worked and no one played.

"This is not good," everybody whispered.

Harcourt Brace School Publishers

TAKE-HOME/KEEP-AT-HOME BOOK

All Smiles

Use with "Pets."

HARCOURT BRACE & COMPANY

by Torré Montero

That's when the frog saw what it needed and it wasn't food and it wasn't water. This frog wanted to go outdoors.

The frog hopped out of the box and into the outdoors.

That was what the frog needed.

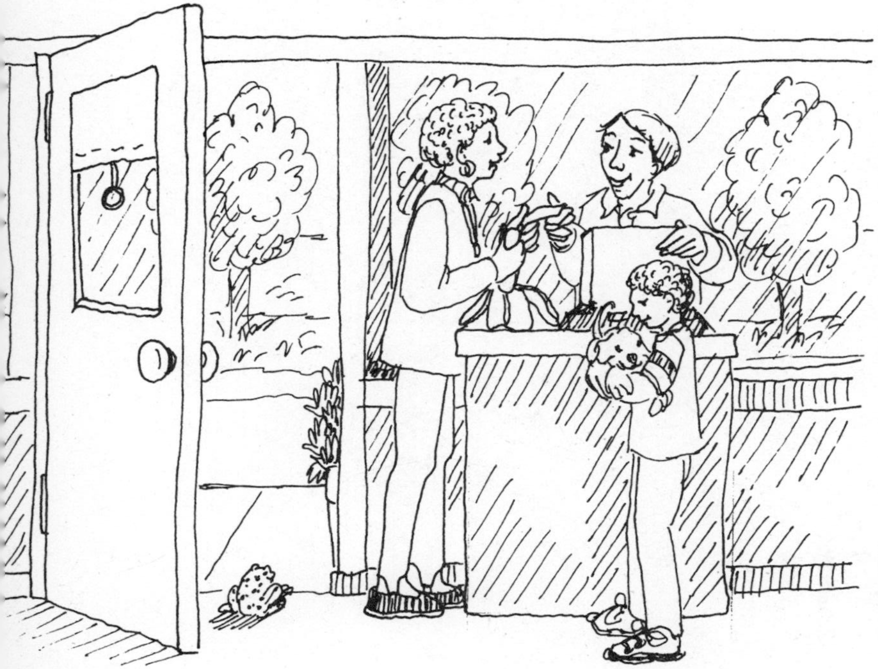

A frog woke up one morning, looked up and then down. Worms and a fly were in the frog's dish. In the frog's box was water, and some rocks to sit on, too.

It was a day like most other days for this frog.

Harcourt Brace School Publishers

The frog could see more animals in the pet shop.
The frog saw a goldfish.

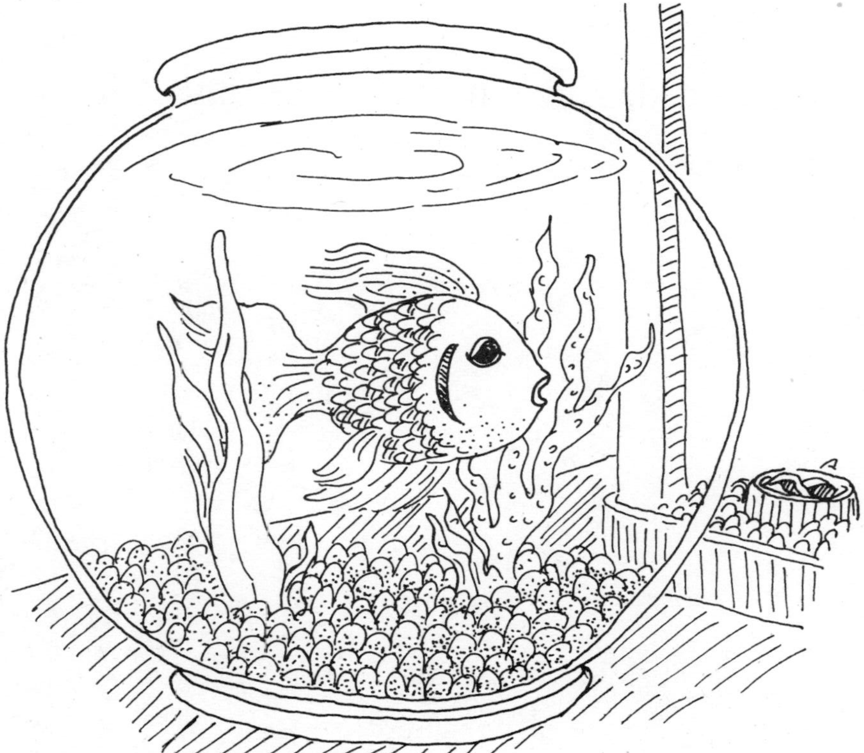

The man stopped what he was doing and got out a dog for the ones who had come in. The dog was the one the boy said he needed.

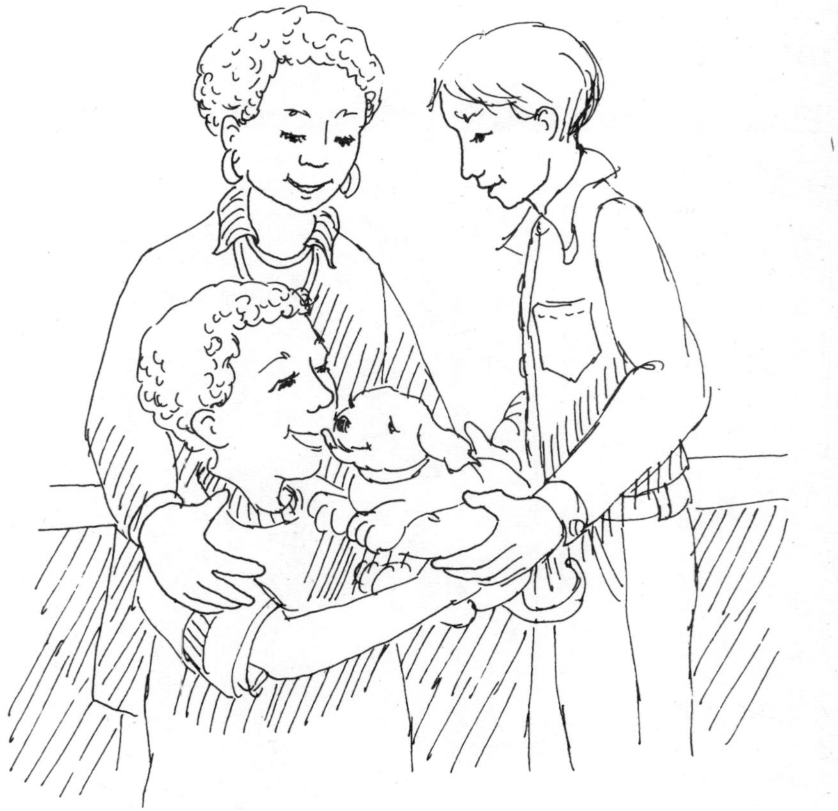

The man opened the box the frog lived in to put in more food. Just then a mother and a boy came into the pet shop. They wanted to look at one of the dogs.

The frog could see a big blue bird, a yellow bird, and a little white one. The birds shouted to everybody.

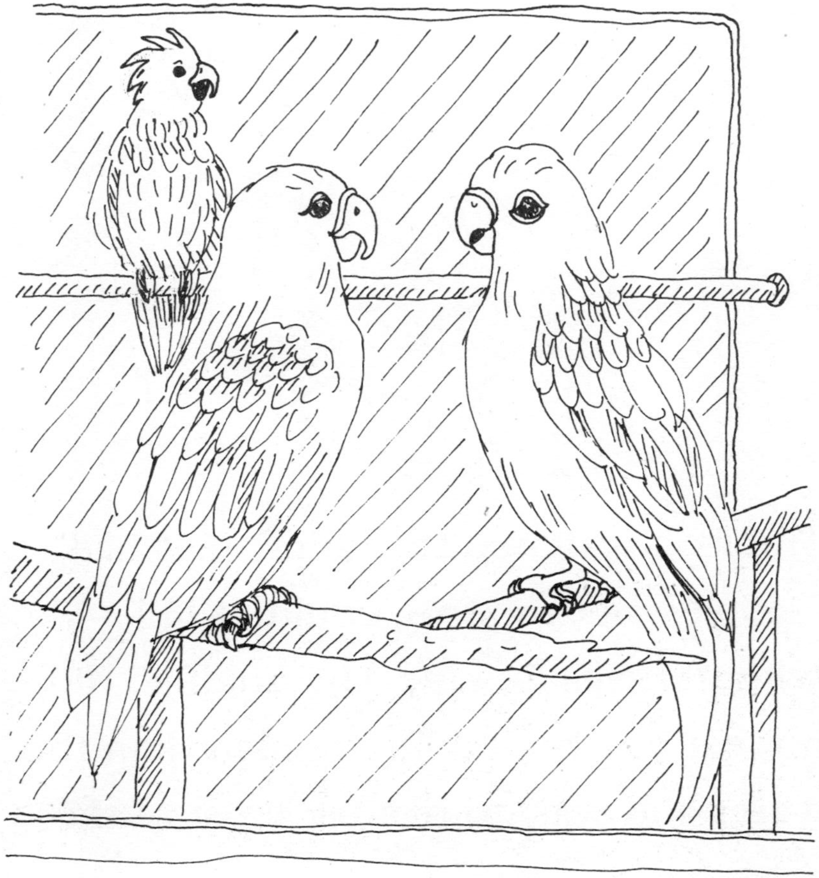

Harcourt Brace School Publishers

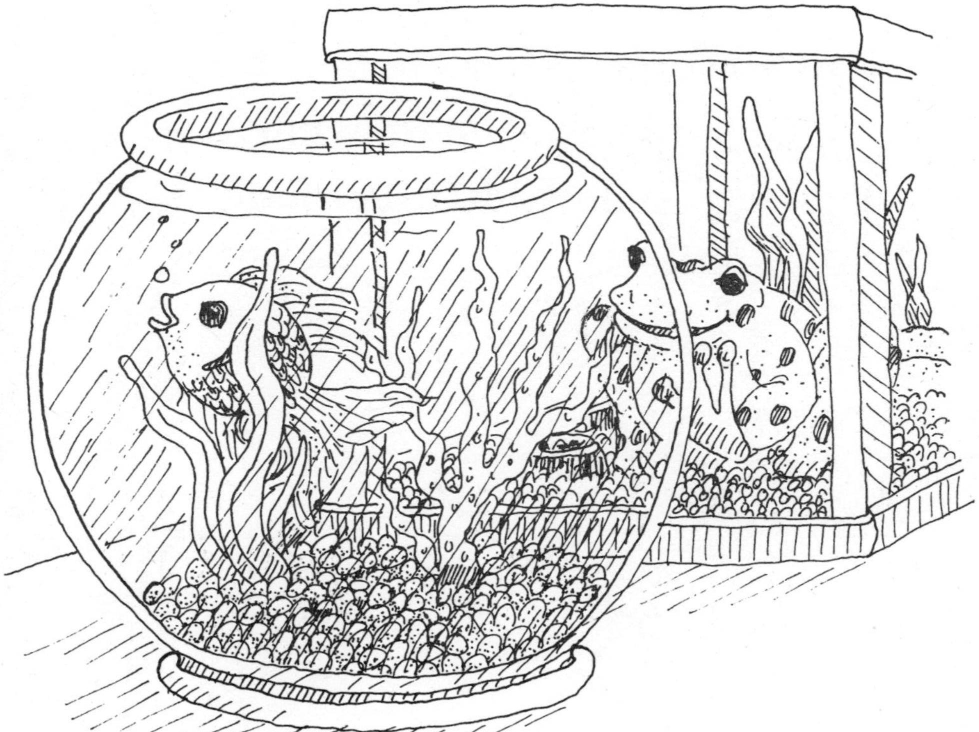

The frog watched the goldfish. It had big eyes, but the frog couldn't tell where it was looking. The goldfish did not eat much food. It was always in the water and was no trouble most of the time.

The man mixed up two kinds of seeds for the birds. He gave them some water, too. The birds began to hop and jump. They lifted up their feet one at a time. It looked like dancing. They had what they needed, too.

Then, he gave the mouse some more food and some wood chips. This was just what the mouse needed.

He gave the goldfish some food. It was just what the goldfish needed.

Then he fed the dogs and cats and gave them more water. The dogs were jumping up and shaking their pen. They were happy to see the man. They had what they needed.

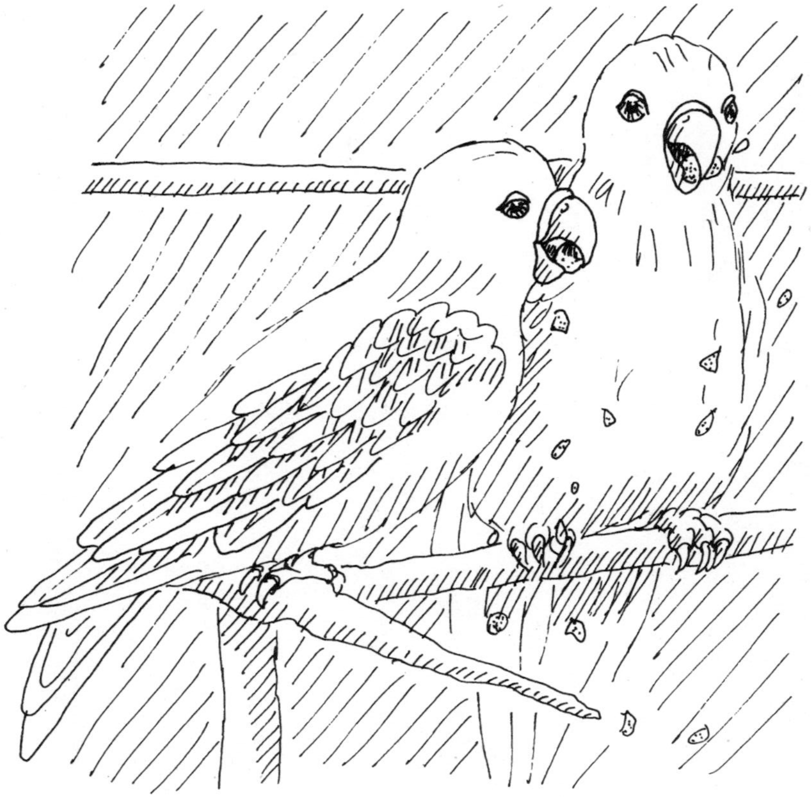

The birds were a lot of trouble. They picked up seeds and cracked them with their beaks for their food. Some of the seeds fell down and made a big mess.

The frog could see other animals in the pet shop. This place also had dogs, cats, and a mouse. The frog saw that the mouse was eating a bit of food with its teeth. Before the mouse was done eating, its cheeks puffed out very big from the food.

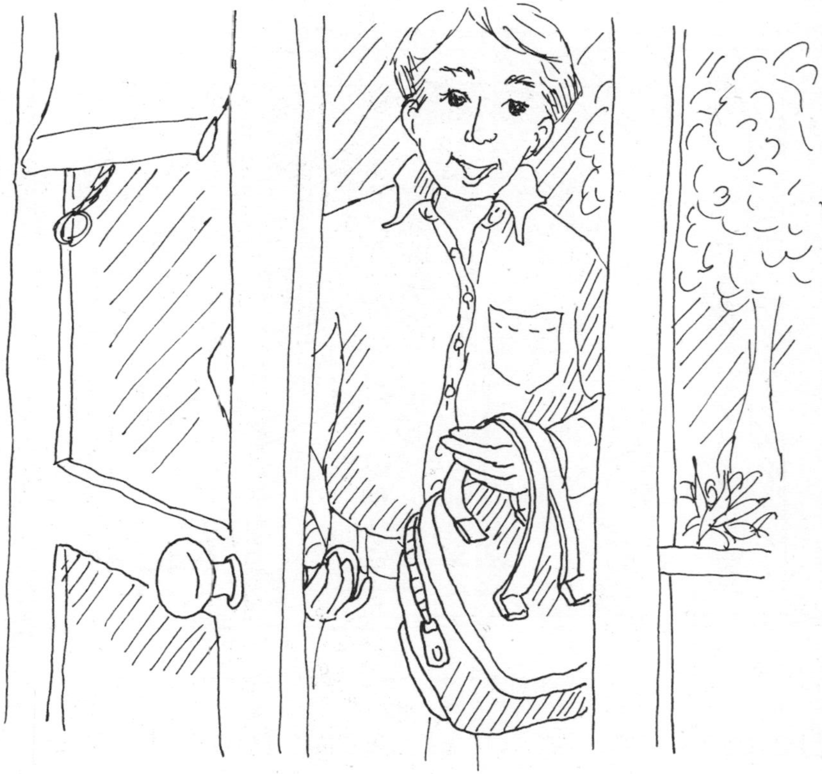

Then in the front, the frog saw a man. This was the same man who came to work every morning. The man came in and put down his bag and his sandwiches.
Then he began to look after the animals.

Harcourt Brace School Publishers

TAKE-HOME/KEEP-AT-HOME BOOK

All Smiles

Use with "The Adventures of Snail at School."

HARCOURT BRACE & COMPANY

The Ship from Space

by Jared Jansen

The green boy got in his
spaceship and blasted it
into space.

What did you think of our story?
What story might you tell?

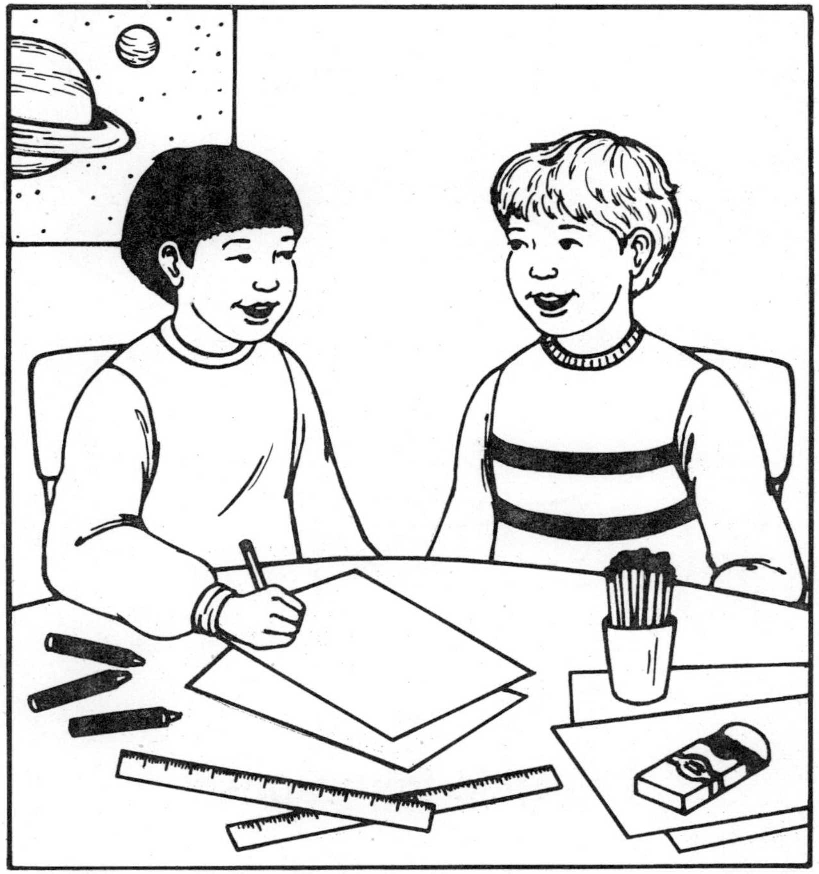

"Let's make up a story," I said to Ned.
"What will it be about?" Ned asked.
"Let's make it about space," I said.
"Good!" said Ned.

The Ship from Space

"Can you make the spaceship?"
I asked Ned. "Yes," he said.
He made the spaceship. This is how
we began our story.

"What time is it?" he asked.
"It's five o'clock," we said.
"Oh, no, I must hurry back. It
is almost time for bed! Father
will be waiting for me!"

“Do you have pets?”
he asked.
“We have pets like these,”
we said.

“What pets do you have?”
we asked.
“I have pets like these,”
he said.

This is what we wrote.

One day a great big
spaceship landed on
the ground.
We were suprised.

All at once, the red door opened. We felt a little afraid. A green boy looked out.

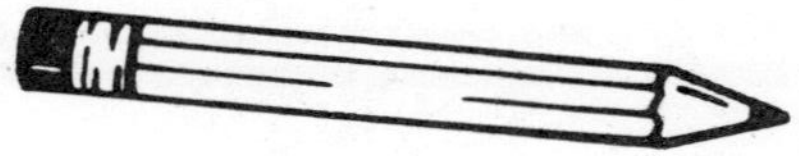

"What do you eat?" he asked.
"We eat food like this,"
we said.

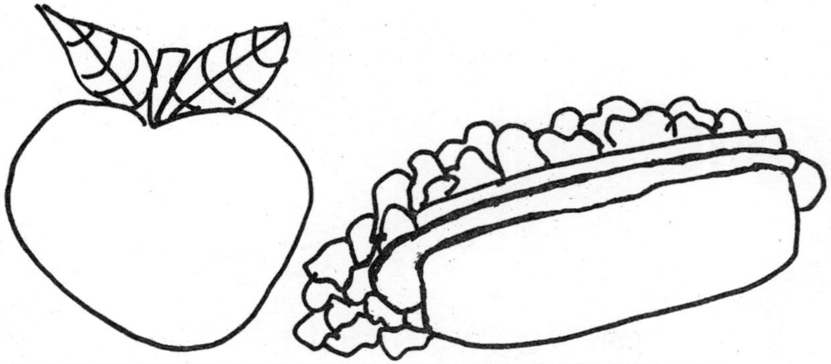

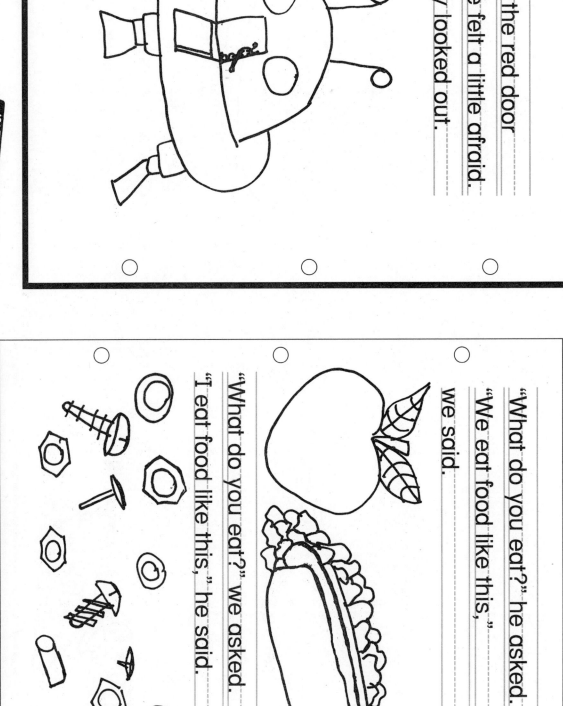

"What do you eat?" we asked.
"I eat food like this," he said.

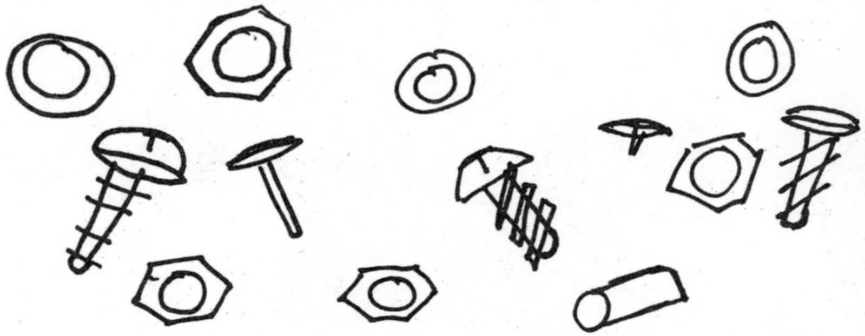

Then the boy looked at me.
"What are you?" he asked.
"I am a boy," I said.
"I am a boy, too," he said.

The green boy had a map in
his hand.
"Please, can you show me
where I am?" he asked.

"May we see your map?"
I asked.
We took the map and looked
at it. It showed all of space.
"You are right here," I said.
"Where have you been?"

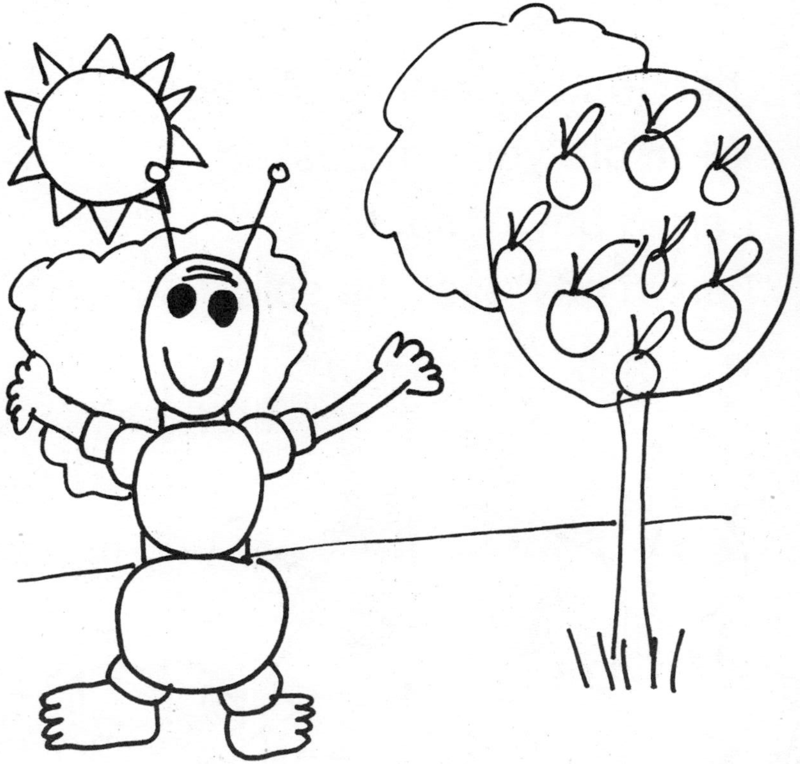

The boy looked up. He put up
his hands.
"I have been all over space in
my spaceship," he said.

Harcourt Brace School Publishers

TAKE-HOME/KEEP-AT-HOME BOOK

All Smiles

Use with "Planets."

HARCOURT BRACE & COMPANY

by Beverley Dietz

Maybe you want to go very, very far away. You might want to visit space and see a star up close. Maybe someday you will!

Let's have some fun. Close your eyes. Think about a place you want to visit. Let's go!

Maybe you want to visit a place that is cold. You could play in the snow and have fun on the ice. You might want to go for a long ride.

You might not want to walk around the city. You could ride in a bus, a train, or a car. The city might be next to water. Then you could see it from a boat.

Do you wish to take a trip to a very big city? You could walk all over and see a lot. Have you been to a big city? Do you live in a big city? What can you see there?

You might want to visit this city. It is very cold there. But not far from the city, hot water comes up out of the ground! This hot water heats some of the houses in the city.

Maybe you want to go to a place that is hot. You might find sand. But you might not find water.

Some big animals live in some hot lands. Would you like to ride on one of them?

Look all around. What is that in the tree? Do you see a big cat coming this way? Watch out!

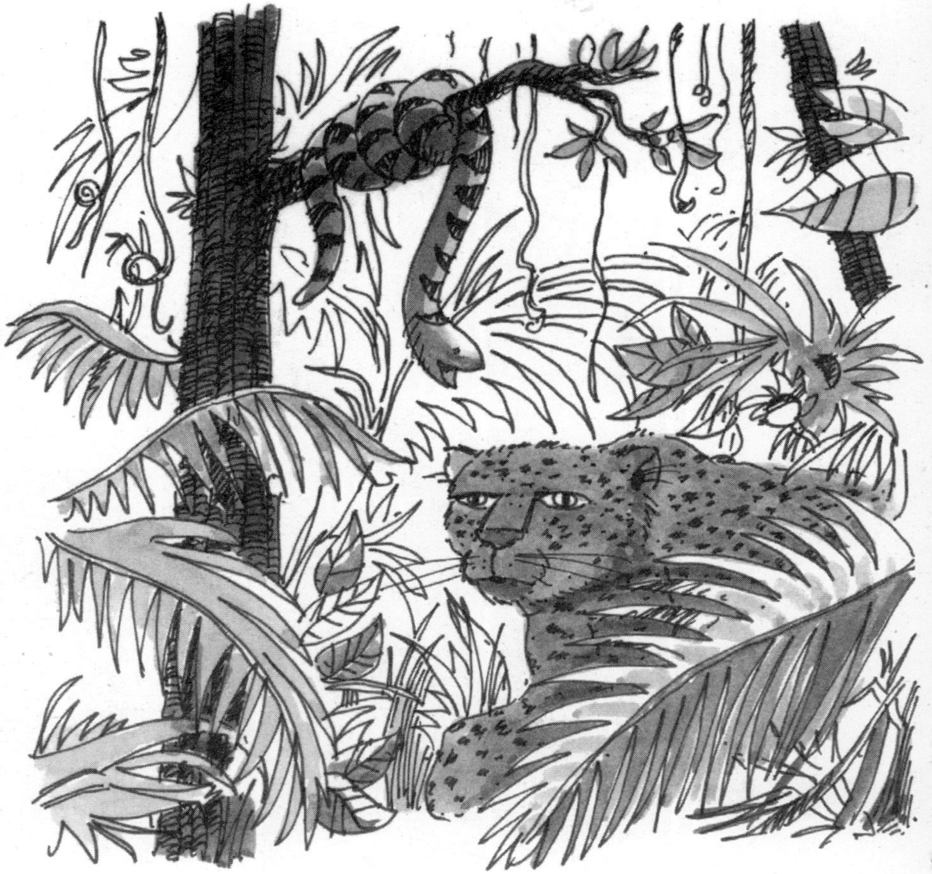

Some places get a lot of rain. Do you wish to go to a place like that? You could see very big trees and many animals.

If you went to visit this city, you could ride the train from one part of it to the next. On the way, you could see trees and gardens right in the city.

Maybe you want to visit a place with lots of open space. You could see horses, too.

You might see lots of animals. Which animal runs fast but can't fly? Which animal can jump very far? Which animal lives in trees and eats leaves?

Harcourt Brace School Publishers

TAKE-HOME/KEEP-AT-HOME BOOK

All Smiles

Use with "Geraldine's Baby Brother."

HARCOURT BRACE & COMPANY

Dancing on the Farm

by Jean Groce

Harcourt Brace School Publishers

"The goat was happy, so that story had a happy ending, Dad," I said.

"It was happy for the goat, but not so happy for me," said Dad. "Every day I had to work with the sheep to keep them dancing. That's why I think the work we are doing is not so bad. It isn't as much work as dancing with sheep!"

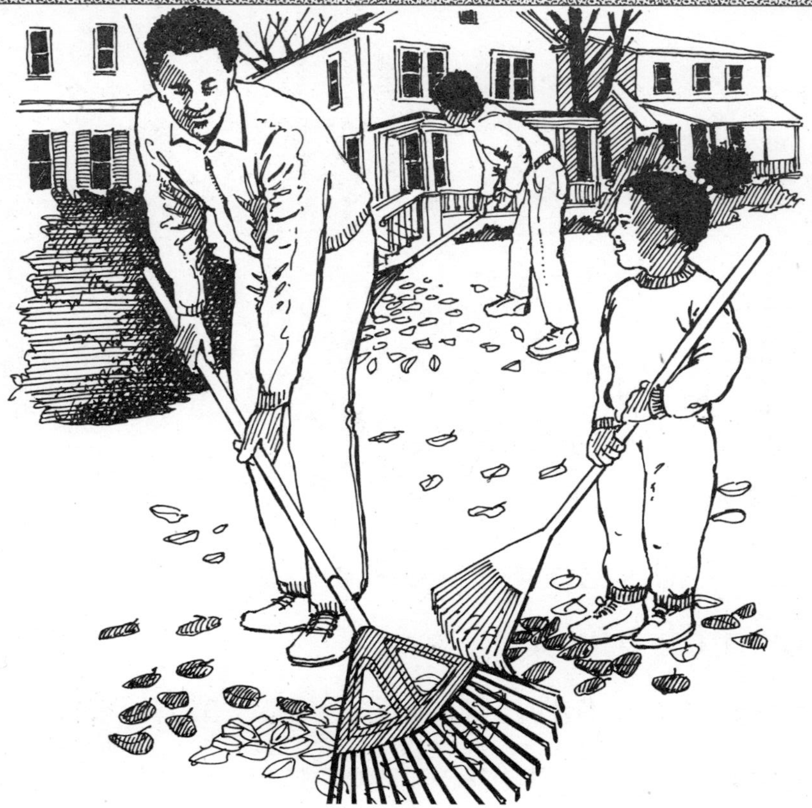

I like to ask Dad about what he did when he was a boy. He can make up a great story!

One day we were working together. "Dad, did you have to work when you were little?" Brad asked.

Dad stopped working and sat down on the step.

"Did I have to work!" he said. "Every day I started working right after breakfast. I didn't stop until it was time for dinner!"

"What did you do?" I asked.

"A little of this and a little of that," Dad said. "I took care of our animals in the morning."

The goat came over to watch. Soon she was dancing right along with the sheep. She looked very happy. From that day on, she and the sheep danced every day. She never did eat up the garden or kick the car again.

That very day my mother took the sheep out behind the house. She showed them some dance steps. It took a while, and I had to help. Before night came, the sheep were dancing!

"Do you mean you fed them?" asked Brad. "That isn't much work."

Dad said, "I fed them, but that wasn't all. I had to help with our dancing sheep, too. Now that was work!"

"Dancing sheep? You had dancing sheep?" I asked.

“Oh, yes,” said Dad. “My mother liked to dance. She showed the sheep how to dance, too. Have you danced with sheep? It’s fun. They always step on your feet.”

“Why in the world did you want your sheep to dance?” asked Brad.

“To keep the goat happy,” Dad said. “A goat that isn’t happy is not very nice to have around.”

“Who will dance with you?” I asked. “You are the only goat we have.”

“I wish you would dance with me,” said the goat.

“No!” I snapped. “I am not going to dance with a goat!”

“Maybe the sheep, then,” the goat said. “Your mother can show them how to dance. Then when they are dancing, I’ll just jump right in.”

I had to say the goat was right, so I asked, "What do you want to do?"

"Dance," said the goat.

"Dance?" I asked.

"Yes, dance," said the goat. "Dancing is fun."

Then Dad said, "That goat was a pet. Some goats make good pets. All that goat made was trouble. She walked across the garden to eat the plants. She ate the hats right off our heads. I felt like screaming the day she kicked our car!"

Harcourt Brace School Publishers

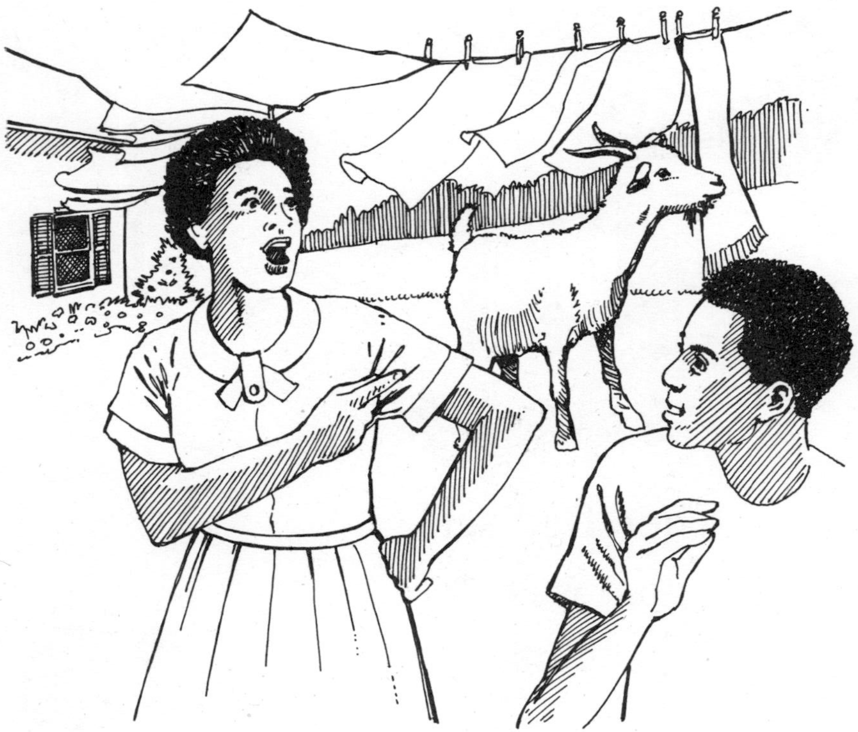

My mother was getting mad. She said I had to find a way to make the goat stop doing all that.

I didn't know what to do. After some time, I sat down and had a chat with that goat.

"Goat, you are making big trouble." I said. "Why are you doing all this?"

The goat stopped eating my mother's scarf. "It's like this," she said. "This place isn't much fun. What can a goat do all day but nap and eat? We goats need our fun, right?"

Harcourt Brace School Publishers

TAKE-HOME/KEEP-AT-HOME BOOK

All Smiles

Use with "Julius."

HARCOURT BRACE & COMPANY

by Susannah Brin

Kate walked over to the swings. She smiled at the boy. She said, "My name is Kate. What's your name?"

"Bill," said the boy. "Do you want to swing with me?" Kate and Bill played for a long time.

Kate was glad she'd wished on a star.

Kate was new in town. Every night she looked out her window and wished on a star. Every night she said,

"I wish I may,
I wish I might,
have the wish
I wish this night.

I wish I could find a friend."

Kate liked to play outside. One day it was too hot to play outside. So Kate went into the house. She walked into her room. Then she stopped. Something scary was on her bed.

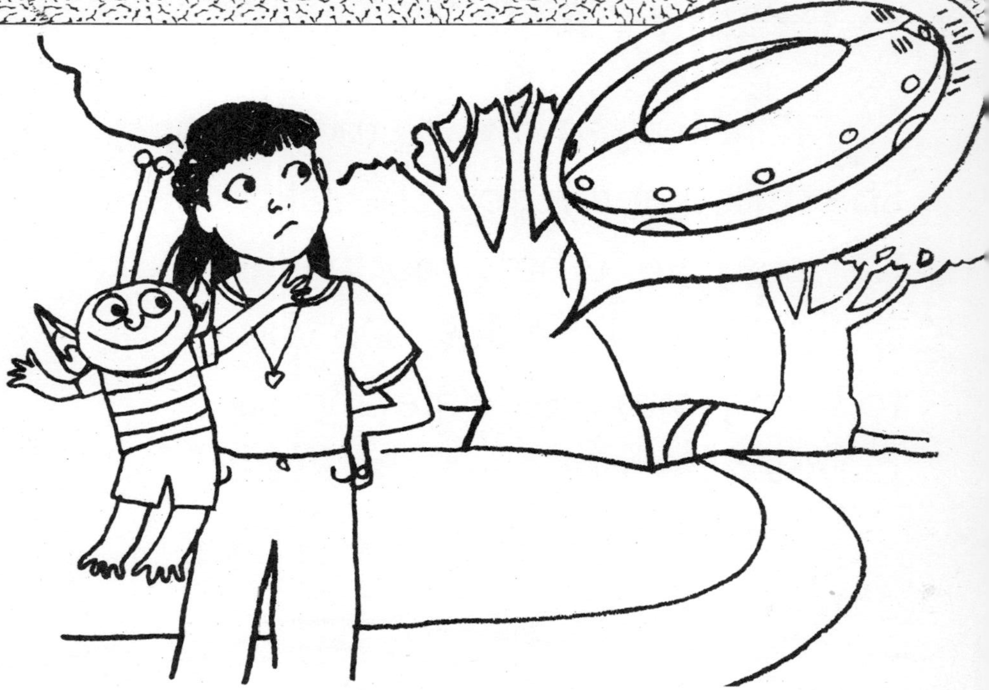

"Will you come with me?" asked Kate.

"No, my work is done. I found you a friend," said Bensun. "I have to go back now."

"Will I see you again?" asked Kate.

Bensun smiled. "When you wish on a star, you'll see me," he said.

Harcourt Brace School Publishers

Bensun and Kate watched the boy swing. "What are you waiting for?" asked Bensun.

Kate looked at her feet. "What do I say?" she asked.

"You say your name. Then you ask him what his name is," Bensun said.

Kate didn't move. She was afraid.

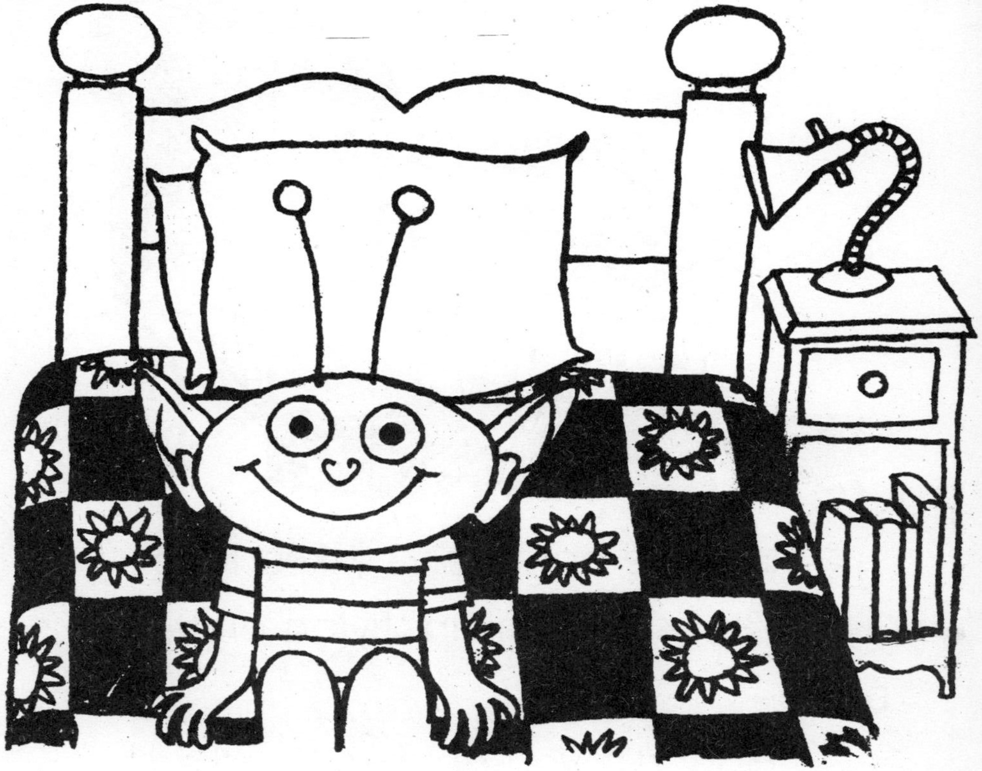

Kate looked again. What she saw was a little being with a big, big head. He rubbed his big eyes.

"Who are you?" asked Kate.

"Bensun," he said. "I live on the star that you wish on every night."

"You live on a star?" asked Kate.

"Yes," said Bensun, flying off the bed.

"How did you get here?" asked Kate.

"In my spaceship. I left it outside," said Bensun, looking around.

"Do you want something to eat?" asked Kate.

"Yes," said Bensun.

Bensun and Kate started back to Kate's house. Then Bensun saw a nice green place with trees and a swing.

"What is that?" he asked.

Kate looked. "That's a boy on a swing," said Kate.

"I think he's the friend you've been wishing for!" shouted Bensun.

"Where is everyone?" asked Bensun.

"They are at home. It's too hot to go outside today," said Kate.

"You don't like the heat?" asked Bensun. He looked surprised. Bensun said he liked the heat. It made him feel as if he were at home on his star.

"What do you eat on your star?" asked Kate.

Bensun smiled. "Ice cubes," he said. Kate gave him ice cubes. He said they tasted good to him.

"What is your star like?" asked Kate.

Bensun said, "It is big and hot."

"Do you have friends?" asked Kate.

"Yes, everyone needs friends."

"I don't have friends," said Kate.

"That's why I'm here," said Bensun, flying around the room. "I'm going to help you find a friend."

Bensun took Kate flying. They went from one end of town to the other end. They saw a dog taking a nap. They saw four ducks swimming on a lake.

Harcourt Brace School Publishers

TAKE-HOME/KEEP-AT-HOME BOOK

All Smiles

Use with "New Shoes for Silvia."

HARCOURT BRACE & COMPANY

by Jeanette Mara

When Rosa got to Donna's house, Donna was waiting.

"Here is a rose for you, Rosa," Donna said. "I'm glad you could visit me."

"I'm glad, too," said Rosa. "I'm glad we are letter friends, and I'm glad we are friends."

At school, Rosa got a letter from her new friend, Donna. Rosa took the letter home to show her mother.

"I'm happy you have a letter friend, Rosa," Mother said. "Do all the children in school get letters?"

"No," said Rosa. "Last week I asked for a letter friend, and today I got a surprise. A letter came for me!"

The trip took a very long time. On the way, Mother said, "Next time, Donna can visit you. She can see your house."

"Do you think she will want to visit me?" Rosa asked.

"Yes," said Mother. "Letter friends always like to visit one another. You just wait and see."

On the day of the visit, Rosa looked pretty. She put on the skirt she liked best. She was happy about seeing Donna. But she knew she had a long ride to Donna's home.

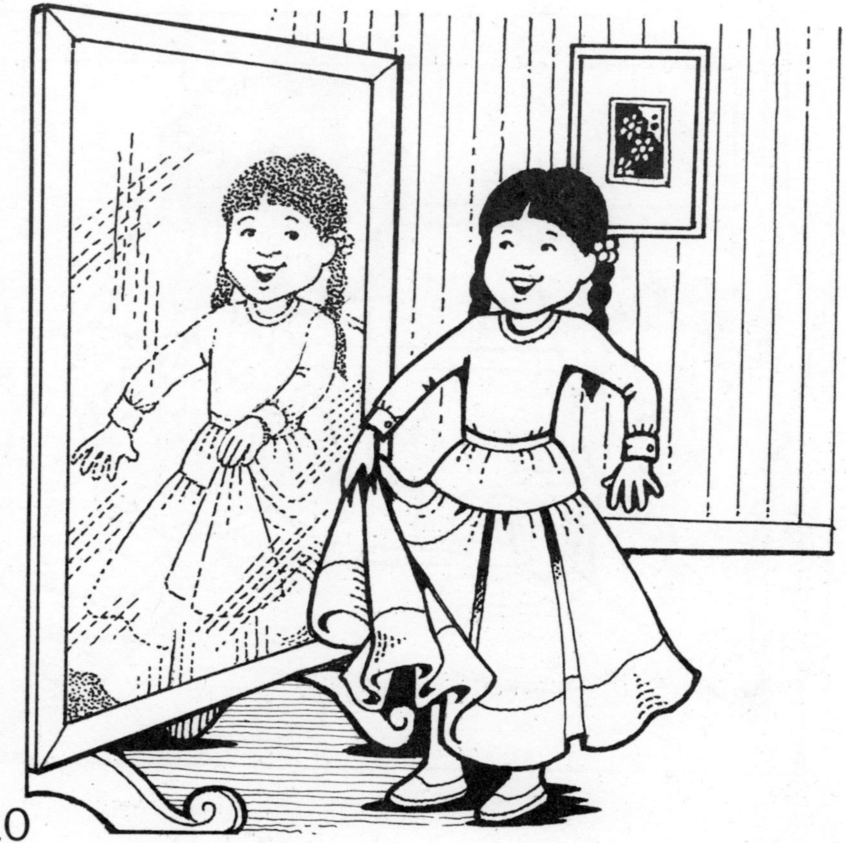

Before bed that night, Mother said, "Think about your letter to Donna. Think about what you want to say. In the morning, we can work on your letter."

Rosa slept. She dreamed about letters to Donna. When Rosa woke up, she felt happy. She had a lot to say in her letter. She wanted to get started on her letter right away.

The next morning Mother surprised Rosa. "I think we can go. I will ask our friends to feed our animals."

"Oh, I'm so happy!" said Rosa. "I'm going to meet my letter friend!"

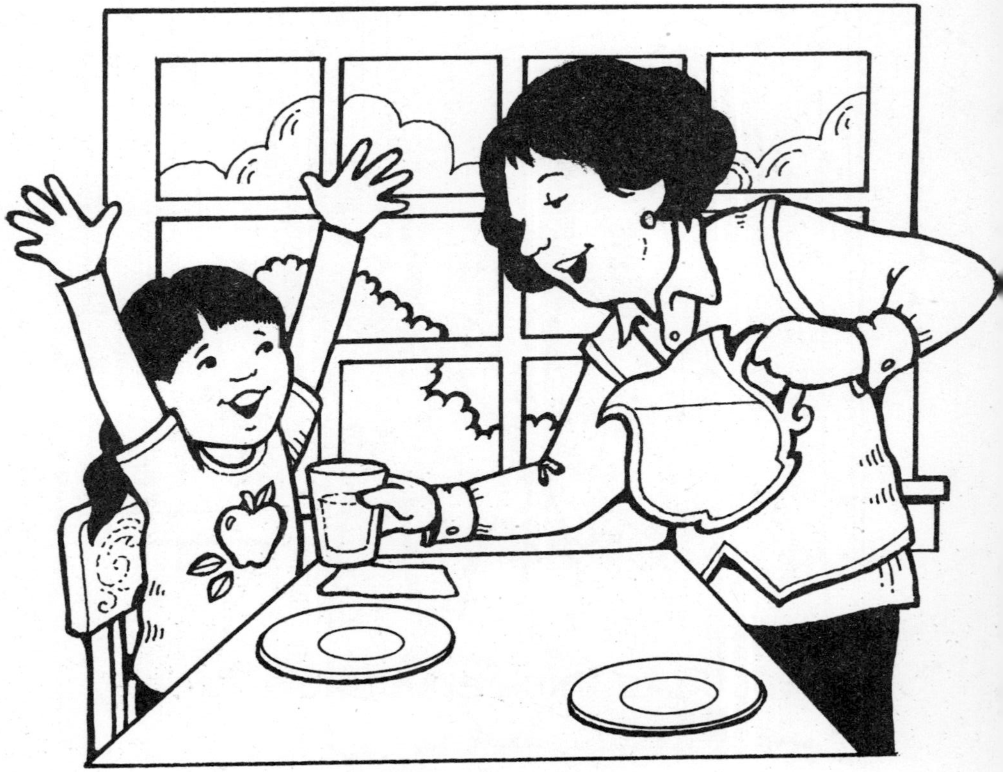

Harcourt Brace School Publishers

Donna lived at the beach. It was far away. Mother needed to get someone to care for the animals. She needed to think about how they could make the trip.

Rosa had to wait for breakfast. Mother was out back, feeding the animals.

When she came in, Mother said, "Let's eat. Then we can start your letter."

DEAR DONNA,
AT MY HOUSE WE HAVE
MANY ANIMALS,

Rosa wrote a nice letter. She wrote about her animals and about her friends at school. When the letter was done, Rosa put it in the mail. She couldn't wait for Donna to write back.

Donna wrote to Rosa again. After that, Rosa and Donna wrote a lot of letters to each other. They were good letter friends. In one letter, Donna asked Rosa to visit her when school was out.